My Sister's
Wishes

My Sister's Wishes

My Promise to Make My Twin's Last Wishes Come True

Melissa Tennant
with Eimear O'Hagan

EBURY
PRESS

3 5 7 9 10 8 6 4 2

Ebury Press, an imprint of Ebury Publishing
20 Vauxhall Bridge Road
London SW1V 2SA

Ebury Press is part of the Penguin Random House group of companies whose
addresses can be found at global.penguinrandomhouse.com

 Penguin
Random House
UK

First published by Ebury Press in 2016

www.eburypublishing.co.uk

A CIP catalogue record for this book is available from the British Library

ISBN 9780091958473

Typeset in India by Thomson Digital Pvt Ltd, Noida, Delhi

Printed and bound by Clays Ltd, St Ives plc

 Penguin Random House is committed to a sustainable
future for our business, our readers and our planet.
This book is made from Forest Stewardship Council®
certified paper.

For Nicole. You are my sun,
my moon and all my stars.

Prologue
July 2013

The light from the laptop's screen bathed my tear-stained face in its eerie glow as I sat in darkness in Nicole's bedroom.

Unable to sleep, I'd crept from my room into hers. I was looking for something, but I didn't know what. Her funeral was in a few hours and I had an overwhelming feeling that there was some final connection I needed to make with my beloved twin sister; one last piece of her I could keep with me before I had to say goodbye for ever.

Looking around the room, it was exactly as she'd left it when she'd been rushed to hospital eight days before. Only now it was silent, the sound of her infectious giggle just a memory. Her collection of stand-up comedy DVDs were stacked neatly on a shelf, and on her dressing table boxes of tablets jostled for space alongside make-up and bottles of nail polish.

In the corner of the room her oxygen tank stood, once permanently by her side, now no longer needed.

Taking her fluffy pink dressing gown from the hook on the back of the door, I wrapped it around me, inhaling the scent of her DKNY perfume. I closed my eyes and, just for a moment, I was transported back in time 14 days, when we had hugged goodbye for the very last time.

'Have a brilliant holiday,' she'd said. 'Don't worry about me, I'll be here when you get back.'

Opening my eyes, my gaze rested on Nicole's bed, neatly made by Mum with its floral print duvet and pillows. As I remembered all the nights we had snuggled up together for bedtime stories when we were younger and, later, to gossip, paint each other's nails and watch movies on her TV, I began to sob quietly.

'I miss you, Nicole,' I said quietly in the darkness, my heart aching.

I knew Mum and Dad were probably wide awake in their bedroom too, but they had their own grief to cope with, and I didn't want them to hear me. I wanted to be alone in these hours, before the sun rose on what was going to be the hardest day of my life.

I don't know why I switched on her computer, or what I hoped to find. Stuck indoors so much because of her illness, the computer and internet had been a huge part of Nicole's life; her lifeline to the outside world. I suppose I hoped it would contain some last piece of her personality, more tangible than the memories in my mind, which I was terrified would fade.

Opening her Facebook account, I took a deep breath and began to read the hundreds of messages people had written on her profile page since her death a week before.

Big, salty tears rolled down my face at the outpourings of love for my sister.

Next, I looked through her photos, chuckling through my grief at a recent one she'd taken of her two dogs, LouLou and Ralph, dressed up in clothes and jewellery. Comforted a little, but still consumed by this feeling there was something more of her there, I almost switched off the computer before spotting a document saved on the desktop.

'My Wishes', it was called.

Puzzled, I opened it and began to read, starting to tremble as I scrolled down the list Nicole must have typed in secret. My heart was thumping so loudly I was sure I'd wake everyone in the house as, one by one, I read my sister's wishes, hearing Nicole's voice in every single word: *Climb to the top of the Eiffel Tower ... Ride a camel ... See the Northern Lights ... Get another tattoo ...* it read.

'It's a bucket list!' I said out loud to myself, completely stunned.

But this was no ordinary bucket list, I realised – these weren't the things Nicole had wanted to do before she died. They were her dreams for when she could start to live properly for the first time. For the day when she received the lung transplant that would free her from the pain and illness of the cystic fibrosis that she'd been born with.

That day had never come, however. She never got the transplant which would have transformed her life and had died exactly seven days ago, without fulfilling a single wish on her list.

She'd talked a lot about her life after a transplant, and all the things she'd do when she was free of the disease, though I'd had no idea she'd actually compiled a list.

Burying my head in my hands, I cried angry tears that my sister had even had to write a list like this. She had been so desperate to live and enjoy life, and she'd never been able to, robbed of her health by her lifelong disease. But then, quite suddenly, my tears stopped as my anger was replaced by an overwhelming feeling of determination.

Nicole hadn't fulfilled her dreams, but could I do that for her? Was this list our last bond as twins, the final step in the journey of our life together? Twenty-one years hadn't been enough, and nothing would change that, I knew. But perhaps knowing I'd been able to at least make her dreams come true would give me some comfort in the years ahead without her.

Looking at the framed photo by her bed of us at our eighteenth birthday party three years earlier, our arms around one another, smiling at the camera, I made a promise there and then to my sister: 'I'll make your wishes come true, Nicole,' I whispered. 'I'll complete this list for you.'

PART ONE

PART ONE

Chapter One

'Action!' I shouted, pointing the camcorder at Nicole.

Clutching a hairbrush in her hand like a microphone, wearing her favourite Cinderella slippers, she twirled around on her bed. 'I'll tell you what I want, what I really, really want …' she sang confidently, flicking her clear plastic feeding tube over her shoulder as if it were a trendy fashion accessory.

I could hardly hold the camera steady I was laughing so much at my sister, always the entertainer of the family. As she spun around, the light caught her copper-coloured curls and her cornflower blue eyes flashed with delight. She looked just like an impish woodland fairy.

It was a rainy Saturday afternoon and, stuck indoors, Nicole and I were making our own entertainment in the bedroom we shared.

'Look at me, I'm a pop star!' Nicole giggled, mimicking the Spice Girls' dance moves perfectly. Strutting up and down the 'stage', she posed and pouted for the camera – before suddenly tumbling off to the side, vanishing completely from view.

'Nicole! Are you OK?' I asked, wincing at the loud *thud* as she hit the carpet.

A few moments later her head popped up over the edge of the bed. 'I'm fine!' she beamed, before we both burst into giggles at her clumsiness. 'We should sell that video to *You've Been Framed*, Melissa. I'd be famous!'

That was my sister Nicole all over. Loud and bubbly, we were only eight years old, and she loved being the centre of attention, never taking herself seriously. But the feeding tube that disappeared up her nose, and her breathlessness, were constant reminders to me that, underneath her chatterbox exterior and ready giggle, my sister was ill.

We were born in Glasgow in October 1991. Our mum, Agnes, was a housewife and our dad, Stewart, was a pipefitter, who often worked hundreds of miles away in the north of Scotland.

Dad worked really hard to support us but we weren't a wealthy family. When we were first born we lived in a tenement flat with two bedrooms in Govan, on the south side of Glasgow. Nicole and I were their first children together, though Dad had two older daughters, Kelly and Laura, from his first marriage, who lived in Southampton. They were 15 and 17 years old when we were born.

Even though twins ran in Mum's family, she says she nearly fell off the hospital bed in shock when the sonographer told her she was expecting two babies at her 12-week scan. Shock soon turned to excitement though, and Mum and Dad saved hard to buy two of everything, and decorate the flat's second bedroom as a nursery for us.

Nicole and I were born on 16 October 1991 – our mum's birthday, as it happens! While I was named after my mum's favourite character in an Australian soap opera, Nicole got her name from the iconic Renault Clio ads, featuring the French girl called Nicole and her 'Papa'.

From the moment we arrived in the world, Mum says she knew we were going to be very different. I was born first, weighing 4lb and, nine minutes later, Nicole was delivered, weighing 3lb and looking, says Mum, just like a tiny doll. But while I was strong and pink, wailing loudly as the midwife swaddled me in a blanket, Nicole was immediately rushed off to the Special Care Baby Unit, as the doctors were concerned because she was so small and having problems with her breathing.

I spent a week in hospital, but it was another month before Mum and Dad were allowed to bring my sister home to join me. It should have been the happiest time of their lives, getting to know their two baby daughters, but as I thrived and gained weight, Nicole was pale and sickly, and her body made a terrible gurgling sound every time she was fed.

We were the third generation of twins on Mum's side of the family, but none of the others had lived: all were stillborn or had died as babies. Mum was terrified this family curse had struck again, her mother's intuition telling her there was something seriously wrong with Nicole.

As the weeks went by, Nicole still wasn't gaining weight and was referred by our family doctor to the Royal Hospital For Sick Children, in Yorkhill, Glasgow, for tests.

Mum's maternal instinct had been right. When Nicole and I were just three months old, Nicole was diagnosed with cystic fibrosis, a genetic condition which clogs up the lungs and digestive system with thick, sticky mucus. People with the disease suffer from infections which damage their lungs, and they can become sicker and sicker as their lung function gets worse. The only thing that helps is a lung transplant; otherwise, people with it will die earlier than those who don't suffer from it.

Because we weren't identical twins I didn't have the condition, but doctors explained it was a potential death sentence for my sister. 'You must both be carriers of the cystic fibrosis gene, which means you have a 25 per cent chance of having a child with the condition,' a consultant told my shell-shocked parents. 'Melissa is healthy, though has a 50 per cent chance of being a carrier too but, unfortunately, Nicole has inherited the condition.'

He had gone on to explain that, in the past, she'd have died in childhood. Luckily, there was much better treatment available when Nicole was a baby, but it would only manage her symptoms and only help to keep her as healthy and strong as possible.

'We can't cure it and, without a lung transplant, Nicole may not live to see her twentieth birthday. I'm so very sorry.'

Mum tells how she gripped Dad's hand tightly as she heard these words, the room spinning. She'd never even heard of cystic fibrosis, but now she was being told this disease had come from her and Dad, and could kill her tiny baby daughter.

That night, Mum and Dad stood over our cots which stood side by side, watching Nicole and me sleeping peacefully.

'I feel so guilty,' Mum whispered, fighting back tears as Dad cuddled her to him. 'She's sick because of us. We passed this disease on to her, Stewart.'

'Don't be silly,' Dad replied. 'How could we have possibly known we carried this gene? It's not our fault. We can't fall apart – she's going to need us to be strong. They both do. This isn't going to be easy for Melissa growing up, either.'

You know when people talk about twins being like peas in a pod? Well, that definitely wasn't Nicole and me. Twin sisters have never been so different: while I was fair-haired and left-handed, she was red-headed (though insisted on being called 'strawberry blonde') and right-handed. When it came to our personalities, we were polar opposites, too. Cheeky and outgoing, Nicole was happiest when all the attention was on her. A bit of a diva, Dad would call her 'the ginger whinger' to tease her, and she always had to be in charge when we played so she could boss me around. She was forever inventing imaginary games and roping me in to play them with her.

Like the time we set up a radio station which we ran from our bedroom, with her as the pop star and me as the presenter.

Pressing 'Record' on our bright pink ghetto blaster which Santa had brought us, I cleared my throat. 'And today's special guest is … Nicole Tennant!'

Nicole launched into her favourite pop song of the moment, hogging the plug-in microphone and not letting me get a word in edgeways. Not that I minded playing second fiddle to her. Even though I was the elder twin, and had walked and talked first, I was much more laid-back, and happy for her to be in charge. Quiet and shy, I was a natural worrier. I thought about things a lot, whereas Nicole was much more forward and boisterous.

I used to be in awe of her confidence. When a new family moved into the street, for example, it was Nicole who marched up to the front door and rang the doorbell.

'Can your kids come out to play?' she'd ask, while I hung back shyly.

And when our extended family came to visit, she'd prance into the living room to sing and dance for them all, while I was content to sit on Mum's knee and watch her perform.

Mum always said we were like chalk and cheese, and yet we were as thick as thieves. Nicole called me La La because Melissa was too hard to pronounce when we were learning to speak, and I in turn called her 'Cole. We were forever finishing one another's sentences.

Our favourite game was School. On a Saturday morning Mum and her mother, Nana, would take us to Govan Market, a bustling selection of outdoor stalls selling everything from clothes to cleaning products. Nicole and I would have saved up our pocket money to spend it all at the stationery stall, buying cheap pencils, jotter pads and marker pens. Back at home, while Mum and Nana had a cup of tea and a natter in the kitchen, we'd transform our bedroom into our very own classroom. We both had an old-fashioned school desk – you know the type with the lid that lifts up? Santa had brought them for us, and we absolutely loved them.

We'd line up all our teddies in front of the desks, as if they were our pupils, then take turns to be the teacher, giving them lessons as we sat at our desks. Although, true to form, Nicole was the teacher more than I was!

At two years old, working as a team, we worked out how to escape from our bedroom, which had a safety gate across the door. I'd lie on the floor and Nicole would stand on my back, and climb over before pulling me over as well.

'You were a pair of little divils,' Mum would tell us, when we'd beg her to tell us the story for the millionth time, delighting in our twin naughtiness.

Our twin bond was so strong, in fact, that we instinctively knew if the other was in pain or upset, even if we weren't together. One time, when we were eight, I was in the kitchen with Mum doing a jigsaw puzzle at the table. Suddenly, I felt a flash of pain across my head and I knew instantly something was wrong with Nicole. 'Where's Nicole?' I asked. 'There's something wrong with her.'

'She's out in the garden with Dad, sweetheart,' Mum replied. 'I'm sure she's fine.'

But I knew, deep inside, that something had happened to my sister.

At that moment, the back door opened and in came Dad carrying Nicole, who had a nasty cut on her forehead.

As Dad explained that she'd fallen over, I immediately rushed over to my sister to hug her and see that she was OK.

'Oh, my God,' Mum said to Dad, clearly shocked at my intuition. 'Melissa knew Nicole was hurt … I've got goosebumps all over my arms. Look!'

But I didn't understand why she was so surprised. It seemed perfectly natural to me that Nicole and I were in tune with one another.

Children are very accepting and, at first, it was just normal to us that I was healthy and Nicole was sick. I grew strong with rosy pink cheeks, but Nicole was short and pale, with a hacking cough.

Trying to protect us, Mum and Dad didn't explain to either of us just how serious her illness was. 'Nicole's got CF,' they would say when I asked what was wrong with her. 'It's nothing to worry about, it just means her lungs don't work as well as yours and she needs special medicine for them.'

And, for a while, I just accepted that; too young to even contemplate my parents might have been keeping the truth from me.

Other children noticed too. 'What's wrong with your sister?' they'd ask me, on the days when Mum wouldn't allow Nicole out to play in the street because it was too cold or wet for her to be out.

'She's got CF,' I'd reply.

'What does that mean?'

'I think it means she's got a bad cough,' I'd answer, not understanding any more than that.

Mum and Dad doted on me and Nicole, and our brother, Gary, 13 months younger than us. Mum had fallen pregnant by accident when we were just four months old, not long after Nicole was diagnosed with cystic fibrosis.

With a one in four chance of having another baby with the condition, she was offered an abortion but refused to even consider it.

'How could I have aborted a baby because it might have had cystic fibrosis?' she said to me years later, when I asked her about it. 'If I'd done that, I'd have been saying Nicole's life was worthless; that she should never have been born either.' She shook her head. 'I decided that what would be, would be. I'd let Nature take its course. And the moment Gary was born, he was so pink and chubby I knew he was healthy, even before they tested him just to be sure.'

Gary was a typical little brother – in other words, full of mischief. As I was naturally placid and calm, he and I rubbed along well together: maybe he sensed he wouldn't get a rise out of me so didn't bother trying to wind me up. When it came to age and maturity, I always felt like I was on an equal footing with Gary, but Nicole and he had much more of a big sister–little brother dynamic, which would grow stronger and stronger as we all grew up. They had what I'd call a rollercoaster of a relationship when we were younger: one day they were best mates, the next they were sworn enemies. If Gary was naughty, Nicole couldn't wait to tell tales on him to Mum; in revenge, he'd play one of his infamous pranks on her. Once, he smeared the toilet seat with Deep Heat cream just before Nicole went to the bathroom. Her yowls as the skin on her bum turned bright red could be heard at the other end of the street!

They loved to wind each other up but underneath the squabbles was a very deep bond. Often Mum would find them snuggled up on the sofa together, fast asleep, after watching one of our favourite Disney DVDs.

With Dad away working for weeks at a time, Mum was often on her own with three young children to look after. And her life was a constant juggling act of caring for Nicole while still finding time for me and Gary.

Nicole had a strict routine of medicines before every meal – the cystic fibrosis meant her body couldn't absorb the nutrients she needed to grow and gain weight – and physiotherapy to clear the mucus from her lungs several times a day. And most of the time it fell to Mum to do all this.

Even a minor chest infection could mean Nicole had to spend a week in hospital hooked up to antibiotic drips, with Mum running between the hospital and home. But she just got on with it. She's one of those very down-to-earth Glaswegian women with endless patience and energy. A spade's a spade to Mum – she doesn't get overly emotional about things. That's always just been her way of coping. If she was ever stressed or tired, we didn't see it.

With a large extended family, there were always aunts, uncles and cousins around to help, thankfully – especially to mind me and Gary when Mum had to take Nicole to her regular hospital appointments. Our Nana was a constant presence in our childhood when we were growing up. Dad's mum developed dementia when we were young, and was in a home, so we didn't have a very close relationship with her, and the rest of his family had either died by the time we were born, or lived down south in Southampton, so it was our mum's family who we were closest to. Nana, a no-nonsense Glaswegian woman just like Mum, was the hub of our large extended maternal family, which included Mum's brother, Jimmy, who was married to Irene and had two daughters called Dianne and Christine; her brother, Joe, who had three sons called John, Joseph and Francis with his wife May; and her brother, John, married to Fiona, parents of Katrina and Paul.

Mum also had a sister, Betty, but she had died aged just 23, long before we were born, and twin sisters who had died at birth.

Nana lived near us and I remember her house always smelled of furniture polish. It was full of heavy, mahogany furniture which was her pride and joy and she'd spend hours polishing it all, roping us in to help when we visited. By way of reward, her kitchen always contained a stash of fizzy drinks and sweets to which we had unfettered access, much to our delight, and she always slipped money in our pockets when we left to go home. She wasn't someone to smother you in hugs and kisses – she was quite reserved when it came to emotions – but we adored her and I could see where my mum got her quiet strength and ability to cope so well with everything cystic fibrosis threw at her.

As well as Nana, our older cousin, Katrina, was always around from the day we were born. She was nine years older than us and when we were babies, she would help Mum care for us, changing nappies and making up bottles. As we got a bit older, she became our babysitter, taking us to the cinema or to the local park, where she taught me, Nicole and Gary how to do handstands and cartwheels.

In fact, Nana, Katrina and the host of our aunts, uncles and cousins were always visiting our house, offering to help Mum and Dad in any way they could – with Nicole's care. And, as I got older, I began to feel flashes of jealousy at all the attention Nicole got, especially because I didn't understand how ill she really was. *Nicole this and Nicole that* ... sometimes it felt like she was all anyone talked about, especially as when family visited they always made a huge fuss of her.

When we were three, Nicole had to spend two weeks in hospital with a chest infection. Watching Mum rush into the house for a quick shower and change of clothes before she returned to the hospital for another night by Nicole's bed in the children's ward was hard, and one day, I began to cry.

'What's wrong?' she asked, gathering me up in her arms and stroking my hair.

'Mum, I miss you,' I sobbed, burying my head in her chest, my tears soaking her top. 'I hardly ever get to see you. You're always at the hospital with Nicole.'

'I'm sorry,' she soothed, wiping away my tears. 'You know I love you just as much, don't you? It's just that Nicole needs me right now.'

As I got older, I just accepted that Nicole needed more of Mum's time. A sensitive wee soul, I didn't want to upset Mum, so tried not to complain.

She'd never known anything else, so Nicole was usually good about sticking to her routine of medicines and physiotherapy.

Sometimes, though, her rebellious streak and longing to be just like everyone else would get the better of her.

Running into our three-bedroom cottage flat which we'd moved to when Nicole and I were one (which was only about two minutes from our first house!), I burst into the living room one afternoon, panting for breath.

'Can she come out to play yet?' I pleaded with Mum, sweaty and excited after a game of tag with the other four-year-olds in our street. 'Please?'

'Not yet. She has to finish her physio,' replied Mum, Nicole lying on her front on the sofa as Mum clapped and pounded her back to clear the mucus.

At that, Nicole looked up at me with a glint in her eye, then suddenly leapt up from the sofa and grabbed my hand. As we ran out of the front door into the blazing sunshine, we were giggling madly.

'Come back, you cheeky pair!' Mum shouted, but she was smiling, knowing there were times Nicole just needed to feel like everyone else her age.

A few months before our fifth birthday, Nicole and I started school at St Jerome's Primary School in Govan. For weeks beforehand, we were fizzing with anticipation – every night we'd lie awake in our shared bedroom, whispering excitedly.

'What do you think our teacher will be like? Kind or cross?' I'd ask. 'I hope she doesn't shout at us!'

'Do you think we'll get to sit together in the classroom?' Nicole would ponder. 'I hope so.'

What we didn't know then, which Mum only told us years later, was that the school had originally wanted to split us up into separate classes. They thought we'd each do better on our own, especially me, because I was the quieter twin. But Mum had point-blank refused, insisting the natural dynamic of our relationship shouldn't be interfered with and that splitting us up would only make us unhappy, not more likely to thrive, at school.

On a sunny morning in August 1996, we walked the short distance with Mum from our home to the school gates, hand in hand, both dressed in navy skirts, blazers and a white shirt and tie. I had blue ribbons in my hair while Nicole had green, and we each had a tartan backpack.

'What's wrong with that little boy?' I asked, as we walked through the school playground, troubled at the sight of a boy our age sobbing and clinging to his mother's legs. 'I don't think he wants to go in,' Nicole said. 'It must be because he doesn't have a twinny to keep him company like we do.'

Looking over my shoulder at the little boy, so upset, I squeezed Nicole's hand and felt grateful I had my sister at my side so I didn't need to feel scared or nervous. I knew that without her I might have been one of those crying children, but her confidence rubbed off on me.

At first, we were a bit of a novelty at school as the only pair of twins in our year, and we soon had a big circle of friends.

Nicole was, unsurprisingly, the alpha girl of the class, always the one who picked the teams for games in the playground, and a real teacher's pet. 'I'm going to tell on you!' was her favourite phrase but, despite being a bit of a tattle-tale, everyone loved her and wanted to be her friend. Even then she had a magnetism, and people wanted to be close to her.

But I didn't mind. I knew I was always her number one friend, and she was mine.

There were times when Mum was forced to be cruel to be kind concerning school, for the sake of Nicole's health, and that wasn't easy for any of us. Like the time when our class at St Jerome's started rehearsing for the end-of-year play: *The Elves And The Shoemaker*.

All the girls were desperate to play the part of the shoe-maker's wife, but it was Nicole and I who were given it to share between us. For weeks, we stayed up late in our bedroom practising our lines and the songs we'd have to sing, so excited about the show. I was more nervous than Nicole about performing, but with her encouragement my confidence grew.

Then, the day of the play, Nicole got a bad chest infection.

'You're not well enough to go into school,' Mum told her that morning, as Nicole coughed and spat phlegm into a tissue, too weak to even get out of bed.

'I can't miss the play! Please let me go!' she wailed.

But Mum stood firm, knowing Nicole wasn't well enough. 'I'll call your teacher and explain,' she said. 'Melissa, you'll have to do Nicole's part for her, as well as your own.'

'I *hate* stupid CF!' Nicole screamed with frustration, burying her head in her pillow in rage.

I left for school upset, knowing how disappointed Nicole was and hating the disease which made my sister's life so hard at times. And even after all the build-up and excitement, I couldn't really enjoy being in the play. As I took my bow at the end, with the rest of my class, all I could think about was poor Nicole stuck at home, missing out once again.

After our first year at primary school, we went on our first foreign family holiday, to Tenerife. Despite the fact that Nicole's health was quite stable at that time, Mum still had to pack a huge suitcase stuffed full of medicines and high-protein milkshakes to make sure Nicole got the nutrients she needed every day.

In the sun and heat, Nicole was much stronger and less plagued by CF symptoms than in cold, rainy Glasgow.

At the side of the swimming pool was a tropical-themed bar, and every day Nicole and I would sit up on the high stools, sipping a fruit juice with a brightly coloured umbrella sticking out of the glass. We thought we were so grown-up, both of us in our neon pink swimming costumes and plastic sunglasses.

Because Nicole was so well on that holiday, Mum was able to relax her strict regime of physiotherapy a little, and give Nicole a bit more freedom than she was able to at home.

'You'd hardly know she was sick out here,' I overheard her say to Dad one day, as they lay on sun loungers while me, Nicole and Gary jumped in and out of the pool at the holiday apartments we were staying at. 'It's so good to see her like this, like a normal child. I wish she could be like this all the time.'

Chapter Two

You know those moments when you look back at your childhood, and realise you'd become a little bit more grown-up? Like when the stabilisers came off your first bike, or you were allowed to go into town shopping with your friends by yourself?

Well, for me, one of those moments was when we were seven, and for the first time ever I properly realised that my sister was very sick.

Walking home from school, I was in a huff. Mum had collected Nicole earlier that day to take her to a hospital appointment, and Nicole had boasted to the whole class she was going to McDonald's as a treat on her way home. I was raging. 'Why does *she* get special treats because of her CF?' I muttered to myself as I stamped into the house.

Walking into the kitchen, I saw Nicole sitting at the table, her face streaked with tears.

'What's that?' I asked, pointing at a plastic tube taped to her cheek, which snaked up her nose one way, and behind her ear the other.

Nicole said nothing, looking down at the table miserably.

'It's called a feeding tube,' Mum answered. 'Nicole's body isn't growing as fast as it should because of her cystic fibrosis. This is just to help her grow up to be a big, strong girl. We'll put special milk in it at night time while she's asleep.' Mum bent down to cuddle my sister. 'Come on now, Nicole. Don't get upset about it.'

Mum was trying to smile but her face looked strained and her voice was wavering. Instinctively, I knew this was something bad. Why did my sister need a tube up her nose to feed her? I'd seen people on TV who were in hospital with them, but they were all really ill. I felt very confused. If CF was just a cough, then why did Nicole need this? Suddenly I remembered hearing Mum on the phone to a friend a few weeks before: '… she's not gaining weight the way she should be. Her body can't absorb enough nutrients. We think she's going to have to be tube-fed …' she'd said. Now it all made sense.

Running over to the kitchen table, I flung my arms around my sister. 'Don't cry, 'Cole. I think it looks cool.'

'Thanks, La La.' She sniffed, rubbing her eyes. 'I think I'm going to call it Sally The Snake.'

That night I lay in bed watching as Mum hooked the machine up to Nicole, the pouch of high-calorie milk flowing through the clear tube and up into her nose.

'Is it sore, Nicole?' I whispered, after Mum had kissed us goodnight and turned off the light.

'No, it just feels a bit tickly up my nose,' she replied. Then she started giggling as the machine started whirring and clunking noisily. 'If I've got a milk machine, does that mean I'm a cow? Moooooooo!'

We fell asleep that night laughing, thanks to Nicole's special gift for seeing fun in just about everything.

Every night after that, I fell asleep to the whirring sound of the machine feeding my sister; a constant reminder that she was ill, even if neither of us fully understood what was wrong with her.

Nicole got used to the feeding tube quickly, flicking it over her shoulder and boasting to other children it was her pet snake called Sally. But using it wasn't always easy.

A nurse would come to our house once a week to change it. One day, I was sitting watching cartoons as the nurse threaded a new tube up Nicole's nose. She then switched on the milk machine to check it was working OK, whereupon Nicole began choking and vomiting.

'It hurts,' she cried. 'Make it stop!'

Mum's face drained of colour as the nurse quickly removed the tube, which had become blocked. It was all over in less than 30 seconds, but it was scary seeing my brave sister so frightened. I cuddled her tightly as the nurse re-inserted the tube, feeling Nicole trembling with fear in my arms.

I got used to seeing her with the tube, but I still hated it. I could see how people stared at her in the street when we went shopping with Mum, and how other children suddenly began to play very gently with her, as if they were afraid of hurting her. In true Nicole style, she loved the attention it got her but all I saw was that it made her different, marking her out as sick. And I didn't like that.

I wanted my sister to be the same as everyone else.

The feeding tube going in was, in fact, just the beginning of a year where Nicole started to need more and more help. We were only six.

She still had to take her medicine every day, have her physiotherapy and now be fed at night by the machine. Next, she had to start using a nebuliser, a machine which makes a mist of medicine which you breathe in through a mask.

One afternoon, a nurse arrived at the house and spent an hour alone with Mum and Nicole in the living room. Gary and I – told to go out and play – instead earwigged at the door, wondering what was going on. When we were finally allowed in, we stopped dead at the sight of Nicole with a clear mask over her face attached by a tube to a plastic box about the size of a shoebox.

She looked like someone from a hospital programme on TV. And it was as if a light bulb had been switched on in my head.

I didn't care how many times Mum and Dad had told me she just had a cough, and cystic fibrosis was nothing to worry about, or how normal they made her medicines and therapy and hospital visits: I knew now there must be something really wrong with my sister. It wasn't normal to have nurses coming to visit, and machines all around the house to feed her and help her breathe.

I was frightened and confused, but I hid how I felt. Nicole was taking it all in her stride and I didn't want to scare her by getting upset:

And, for the first time, I started to notice that Mum was acting differently too. She'd always been so unfazed by Nicole's care, never making a big deal of it, but now I would see an anxious look quickly flash across her face when Nicole had a bad coughing fit.

'What's wrong, Mum?' I'd ask. 'Are you worried about Nicole?'

'No, no, darling, don't be silly. There's nothing to worry about. Off you go and play,' she'd reply, plastering a smile on her face as she shooed me out the door.

But I'd always been the intuitive twin, and I knew she wasn't telling me the truth.

Later that year, Nicole and I made our First Holy Communion at St Constantine's Roman Catholic Church, in Govan, which was where we had been baptised. Our whole class was to make it on the same day and for weeks before it was all anyone could talk about.

'We're getting our dresses made by a dressmaker,' I boasted to our friends, as we played in the playground at lunchtime.

'And we're having a *massive* party afterwards,' Nicole chimed in.

It was the most exciting thing that had ever happened to us and we spent hours every day after school drawing our dream dresses with felt-tip pens, plastering our bedroom walls with our efforts.

A month before the big day, Mum took us to the home of a local dressmaker to be measured. We were so excited we could hardly stand still as she passed her tape measure over us.

The day before the church service, Mum's hairdresser put our hair in rollers in the salon. We felt so grown-up! Walking home, we skipped ahead of Mum holding hands looking, she said, like two wee old ladies with our heads covered in rollers and tied up in headscarves.

That night we barely slept a wink, too excited.

'Can we put our dresses on yet?' we pleaded with Mum, as she finished Nicole's physiotherapy the next morning.

'Yes, let's get you two dressed. We don't want to be late to the church,' she replied with a smile.

I remember so vividly standing with Nicole in front of the mirror in our room, both in our identical dresses. Reaching to mid-calf, they had been made in white satin, and had short, puffed sleeves trimmed with delicate lace. Our curled hair was pinned half up, and we each carried a little prayer book and a set of children's rosary beads.

'We look like princesses, La La,' Nicole whispered, a massive smile on her face.

At the church, the class lined up in pairs to walk up the aisle to the altar and take Communion for the first time. But while all the other girls were paired with boys, our teacher placed Nicole and me side by side.

'I wanted to walk up with a boy,' Nicole whispered to me as waited our turn at the back of the church, pouting with disappointment.

I nodded in agreement, but secretly I was pleased my sister and I were going to share such an exciting moment. I was never happier than when she was by my side. And, as we knelt at the front of the church together, after taking Communion and being blessed by the priest, I fervently made a silent prayer: 'Dear God, please make my sister better, and take away her CF for ever. Thank you, from Melissa. Amen.'

After the mass, Mum and Dad threw a big party for all our family and friends at a local function room. We couldn't believe it as five- and 10-pound notes were pressed into our hands by relatives!

'We're rich, Nicole!' I squealed as, afterwards, we counted all the money we'd been given. 'I'm going to buy a pink TV with my money, for our bedroom.'

'I'm going to buy a new bike with ribbons on the handles and a basket,' she replied. 'I've wanted one like that for *ages*.'

That night we lay in bed exhausted from all the fun, but too hyped up to sleep.

'Next time we're in a church in a white dress, we'll be brides,' I whispered to Nicole. 'I'll be your bridesmaid, and you'll be mine, OK?'

'It's a deal, sis,' she whispered back.

It never crossed our young, innocent minds that Nicole might not live to experience a wedding day, and that our Communion would be the only time in her life she would walk up the aisle of a church in a beautiful white gown.

Just a couple of months later, Mum and Dad called us both into the living room one evening. I knew instantly something was up, they looked so serious.

'You know how sometimes you have to go into hospital when you're not well, Nicole?' Mum said. 'Well, your doctors there have decided they'd like you to go and see them a bit more often, even when you're not poorly.' Nicole and I looked at each other. 'They want to keep you feeling well, so every two months you're going to spend two weeks in hospital with all the doctors and nurses you already know, so you can have some extra feeding and medicine. How do you feel about that, pet?'

The room was silent.

'Am I getting sicker?' Nicole asked so quietly, I could barely hear her.

'No, darling, but the doctors would like you to grow a bit bigger and taller, like your sister. And seeing you a bit more will mean they can hopefully stop you getting as many chest infections and colds like you do now. Now, doesn't that sound good?'

Nicole nodded hesitantly. 'Will I still get to see Melissa every day?' she said.

'Every single day,' Dad replied. 'We promise.'

None of us knew it then, but that was the beginning of eight years' worth of two-week hospital stays every two months for Nicole.

Despite her night feeds, Nicole remained underweight because her body still struggled to absorb the nutrients it needed to grow. Doctors wanted to hospitalise her regularly so they could give her even more artificial feeds, as well as other medicines to keep the chest infections to which she was prone at bay.

And so, just as her physiotherapy and night-time feeds had become part of our family routine, so too did her hospital stays.

Nicole was always admitted on a Monday, so on the Sunday night she got ready. As Mum ironed a pile of clothes and pyjamas to last her the fortnight, Nicole and I would pack her pink suitcase in our room.

'I want my board games and my teddies, and my favourite duvet covers,' she said, determined each time to transform her hospital room into a little piece of home. 'You're so lucky, Melissa,' she would sigh. 'I wish I was normal like you.'

When she said things like that I felt guilty. I didn't want to be sick like Nicole, but it wasn't easy being healthy when your twin wasn't the same as you.

And those Monday mornings were always the same: from the moment she opened her eyes Nicole was grumpy and quiet, knowing the clock was ticking down towards two weeks of tube feeds, IV drips full of antibiotics and intensive physiotherapy.

At first, doctors hadn't wanted her to go to school during the day, but Mum had insisted. 'I'm not having her feeling any more different to her sister and friends than she already does,' I overheard her saying to a doctor outside Nicole's hospital room one day. 'I want her to have the same chances in life, not to fall behind everyone else just because she has this disease.'

So, every morning a taxi brought Nicole to school, and when the bell rang at 3 p.m. Mum would be waiting to take her, as well as Gary and me, back to the hospital.

With Dad away working, we had to go too because there would be no one at home to look after us.

Mum would do Nicole's physiotherapy and get her back into her pyjamas, then me, Gary and Nicole would do our homework, watch TV and play games. At about 5 p.m. a trolley would come round with Nicole's dinner on it – Mum would cook Gary's and my tea in the ward kitchen. And at 8 p.m. we'd go home, kissing Nicole goodnight before we left.

The children's ward soon became as much my second home as Nicole's. I knew all the staff and could tell from the colour of their uniform who was a nurse, who was a doctor and who did what. 'Hi, Melissa!' they'd say to me as they did their rounds. 'How's your sister today?'

Nicole wasn't the only long-term CF patient at the hospital. There were three other children her age with cystic fibrosis who were also in every few months: Holly, Gaynor and Stuart. They had soon become a little clique – playing together, falling out and making up all the time.

Gaynor was Nicole's closest hospital friend. The same age as we were, I knew how much Nicole valued having someone her age who knew exactly what she was going through. Gaynor was very like Nicole – feisty and mischievous – and together they had quite a reputation for being the troublemakers of the children's ward! I didn't feel threatened by their friendship, understanding that Nicole needed her 'sick friends' as much as her healthy ones, because that reflected the two halves of her life, in a way; but I quickly started to dread her hospital stays as much as Nicole did as, for those two weeks, family life was turned on its head.

I'd arrive at school every morning and immediately start watching the clock, waiting for my sister to arrive from hospital. Often Nicole was late because her morning physio over-ran or her taxi got stuck in traffic.

'Is your sister coming in today, Melissa?' the teacher would ask me, and I'd feel stressed because I wouldn't know. And then Nicole would come bursting into the classroom, flustered and upset because she was late again.

MELISSA TENNANT

Although I never complained, there were days after school when I just wanted to go home or go to a friend's house to play, instead of having to spend hours in the hospital with its funny antiseptic smell. And I'd feel guilty again, just thinking like that. I knew I only had to go for a few hours, while Nicole had to spend weeks at a time stuck there.

The worst part, though, was going to bed every night alone in the room we shared. It always felt wrong – the room was too quiet without Nicole. We always spoke on the phone every evening before bedtime, singing a little song we'd made up to one another: '*I love you, my sister. And we will never be apart. Never, ever be apart!*' But it just wasn't the same as having her in the bed beside mine. I'd lie awake in the dark, afraid to go to sleep because if I had a bad dream she wouldn't be there to climb into my bed and tell me funny stories until I fell back to sleep.

'Night, night, sis,' I'd whisper, after Mum turned the light off, knowing Nicole was doing the same from her hospital bed across the city.

Until we were 10 we had quite a distant relationship with our half-sisters from Dad's first marriage, Laura and Kelly, who lived hundreds of miles away in Southampton and were 20 or so years older than us. There was no Facebook or Skype back then like there is now. So they would visit us once a year and the rest of the time we relied on phone calls at Christmas and birthdays, and cards, to stay in touch. And so when Mum and Dad asked me, Nicole and Gary if we'd like to go and stay with them for a week, flying down by ourselves, I had mixed emotions. I was excited when it was decided that we would go, but also a bit nervous because we didn't know them that well, even though they were our sisters.

Secretly, I was also anxious about being away with Nicole without Mum or Dad there. What if she got ill and Laura and Kelly didn't know what to do? I kept my worries to myself though, not wanting to cast a shadow over Nicole and Gary's excitement.

Mum and Dad walked us as far as the departure gate at Glasgow Airport but, as they kissed us goodbye, I burst into tears. It was the first time I'd ever been away from home without them, and suddenly I felt scared about getting on a big plane and going to stay in a strange city for a whole week.

'You are *so* embarrassing,' muttered nine-year-old Gary, walking off into Departures, not wanting to be seen with his snivelling sister.

'You're being daft, Melissa!' Nicole laughed. 'We're only going away for a week! Come on, and stop being such a baby!' Taking me by the hand, she pulled me through the departure gate, where an air hostess was waiting to walk us onto the plane.

As soon as Laura and Kelly met us at the other end, I immediately relaxed. It was strange – although we hadn't spent that much time together as siblings, there was a bond between us all. It felt really natural and easy being with them, and my nerves disappeared.

We stayed with Kelly and her husband, Gareth, and baby son, Henry, at her house in Southampton; Laura lived nearby. Mum had packed plenty of high-protein shakes for Nicole, and Kelly had visited the local children's hospital to get advice before we'd arrived so she was clued up on how to look after Nicole and do her physio every day.

We had a brilliant week shopping, going to the cinema and out for meals – just getting to know our sisters better. But, on the last day, Nicole had a bad coughing fit and began to spit up blood.

This wasn't unusual, but it wasn't the sight of the bright red blood in the tissue she held to her mouth that frightened me. It was how scared Laura and Kelly clearly were.

We were used to Mum or Dad just dealing with things like that calmly, as if it was no big deal. Kelly, though, understandably panicked and insisted on taking Nicole to hospital to be checked over, while Gary and I waited with a very anxious Laura at her house. It hammered home to me how much of a protective bubble there was around all three of us, created by Mum and Dad in their determination to make sure we all felt life was as normal as possible, despite Nicole's illness.

Seeing Laura and Kelly so worried really unsettled me and, even though it had been a lovely week, I felt really relieved to get home the next day, back to the people who knew best how to look after Nicole.

Chapter Three

Sitting at the breakfast table, both in our brand new uniforms, Nicole and I beamed at one another with excitement. It was 1 September 2003, and we were off to 'big school' for the first time.

'I can't believe my baby girls are starting secondary school. Time flies too fast, eh?' Dad said, ruffling our carefully plaited hair as he sat down at the table with us and began to read his paper.

'We're not babies, Dad!' Nicole laughed. 'We'll be teenagers soon!'

'I wish you could always stay my babies,' Dad replied, a sad expression on his face.

'Don't you want us to grow up?' Nicole asked.

'Of course I do. Don't pay any attention to a silly old man like me,' he replied, smiling.

But that sad look was still in his eyes and I didn't understand it. Why didn't he want us to become adults?

As we gobbled down our cereal, Mum put our packed lunches in our new school bags, which were crammed full with fancy new pens and jotters. Nicole was chattering nonstop about the new subjects we were going to be studying, and giggling about which new boys might fancy her.

'I think I'll be best at History,' she said. 'And you'll be best at Maths. I just hope we don't get loads of homework!'

I joined in, but underneath my excitement I felt a bit sad. Because, for the first time in our life – apart from when Nicole had been in hospital – we were going to be apart.

It was traditional for the children at our primary school to go on to Trinity High in Renfrew, a Catholic secondary school 25 minutes by bus from our house. Our whole class was going there, and I couldn't wait. New subjects, a smart new uniform, making new friends ... it all felt so exciting. But Nicole had decided she didn't want to follow the crowd; she wanted to be different, and had applied to go somewhere else. So she was off to Govan High, a non-denominational school which was a 10-minute walk away.

Now, I was off to the bus stop in my black and green uniform, while Dad was driving her the 10-minute journey in her black and red uniform.

Starting secondary school felt like such a milestone, but not sharing it with Nicole had taken the shine off it a bit for me.

'Why don't you want to go to the same school as me anymore?' I'd asked her weeks before, when we'd filled in our application forms with Mum.

'Don't be upset, Melissa. I want to be just "Nicole" for once – not always "Nicole and Melissa".' She looked at me. 'And no one at Govan High knows me, so they won't know about my cystic fibrosis. I can start with a clean slate there.'

By now Nicole's feeding tube, which had gone up her nose, had been replaced with one which was inserted straight into her stomach, under her clothes, so it was much more discreet.

'I won't be "Nicole who's always sick",' she continued. 'Well, not at first anyway – when they find out I stay over in hospital for two weeks every two months, that might be a bit of a giveaway,' she said wryly.

I felt sad, but I understood where she was coming from. The previous year, I'd taken up Irish dancing as a hobby, something in which Nicole wasn't interested, or well enough to do, even if she had been. Three evenings a week I'd spent two hours at my dance lessons at a local community hall, learning the intricate steps, practising, getting dressed up in a fancy costume and going to competitions at the weekend. I loved it!

Of course my costumes and dancing shoes were usually second-hand, but I didn't mind that, as I knew that with just one wage coming in, and three children to look after, sacrifices had to be made. It was an expensive hobby, what with the cost of lessons and costumes, and the travelling to competitions, but Dad worked hard as a pipefitter, still often going away for weeks at a time up to places like the remote Shetland Islands, to make sure we didn't have to go without as a family. I missed him so much when he was away – we all did. But I felt proud to have a dad who worked so hard for us all so we could have the same things as other children, and I could have hobbies like my dancing.

My *Riverdance* DVD was on constantly and I practised my steps at every opportunity – in front of our bedroom mirror and out in the street. It was my first real experience of doing something myself and not as a twin. At home I was used to Nicole being the centre of attention but on a stage, as I kicked my legs high in the air, it was all about me. And while I never told anyone, I secretly enjoyed the time away from the house where so much revolved around Nicole's health. At times I felt forgotten about because so much of everyone's attention was taken up with her. I knew it wasn't her fault, though – she'd have swapped places with me in a heartbeat just to be normal and well.

And, despite loving my hobby and relishing the attention, I still missed my sister – I wanted to look out into the audience and see her there clapping for me; instead, I knew she was stuck at home or in hospital, and that cast a cloud over every performance I did.

The competitions I took part in were often a long way from Glasgow and meant I was away for a whole weekend. I was too young to travel alone, and Mum could never take me because she needed to be with Nicole at home, so I always went with my older cousin, Dianne, and her daughter, Rhiannon, who was also an Irish dancer.

The night before I went, I'd be full of excitement and nerves, and Nicole always gave me a homemade good-luck card to take with me. 'I wish you could come with me,' I said one Friday evening, as I carefully packed my fuchsia-pink and royal blue dancing costume. 'We're staying in a hotel and loads of the other girls will be there. It's going to be brilliant.'

'I wish I could, too,' Nicole answered wistfully. 'Sounds like much better fun than being stuck at home.'

One weekend, Dianne, Rhiannon and I travelled down to Bournemouth for a national competition, held at a holiday park in the area.

Mum waved us off, hugging me tightly. 'Good luck,' she whispered. 'I so wish I could be there but Nicole needs me. You understand, don't you?'

''Course I do, Mum,' I said, hugging her back. But, inside, a little part of me wished that just once she could see me dance.

'Good luck, La La,' Nicole said, giving me a huge hug. 'Knock 'em dead with your fancy footwork!'

The next day, I came first in my age group at the competition, after dancing my heart out. Standing on the stage waiting to be presented with my medal, my eyes filled with tears. I'm sure people watching thought they were happy tears because I'd won, but the truth was I wanted so badly for Mum and Nicole to be there to see me. Just once.

Walking off the stage, the other girls who had won medals were all hugged by their mothers and I felt a stab of jealousy.

'I won, Mum,' I said on my mobile phone, because she always insisted I call her with any news. 'I wish you could have seen me.'

'Oh, Melissa. I wish that too, sweetheart. So, *so* much …' she replied sadly.

And so, enjoying my Irish dancing as time to just be me, I couldn't be angry with Nicole for wanting to go to a different school. I knew what it was like to want to be your own person for once, and not always half of a twosome. While I was going to miss her, I was happy that for once she had an opportunity to feel a bit independent.

A couple of months into that first year at secondary school, everyone in my English class had to make a speech about their hero.

'I'm going to talk about Nelson Mandela,' one boy said.

'Well, I'm going to do Mother Teresa,' said a girl. 'Who are you going to do, Melissa?'

The moment we'd been given the assignment, I'd known instantly who I'd talk about. There was just one true hero in my life.

'I'm going to talk about my sister,' I replied.

Some people in the class knew Nicole from primary school and understood instantly why I'd chosen her as my hero; but I knew that for others, it would be the first time they heard about the disease my sister lived with every day.

The night before we were due to make our speeches I sat up late, long after everyone had gone to bed. Hunched over the kitchen table, I carefully wrote and rewrote my speech, determined to make people understand just how amazing my sister was.

The next day I stood in front of the class, my legs shaking with nerves as all faces looked at me expectantly. Swallowing hard, I started speaking, quietly at first; but then I thought about Nicole and how brave she was. I forgot that everyone was watching me and began to talk. 'My twin sister Nicole takes 40 tablets a day. She can never be spontaneous because every day of her life revolves around physiotherapy and medicines. She's had more needles stuck in her than I've had hot dinners and she spends at least a quarter of the year in hospital. She has a disease called cystic fibrosis which means her lungs don't work properly, and she can't even walk to school because it would leave her gasping for breath. Nicole is the strongest, bravest person I know, and rarely stops smiling. And one day doctors *will* find a way to cure her so she can live a normal life. She's my hero.'

As I walked back to my chair the room was silent. Sitting down, I looked up and saw that the teacher had a solitary tear rolling down her check. 'That was beautiful, Melissa,' she said. 'Well done.'

And at that, the class began to applause and cheer.

Blushing like mad I laughed and shushed them, but inside I felt so happy that now even more people knew how incredible my sister was.

At the end of our first year at secondary school, Nicole decided she wanted to transfer to mine.

'I thought you wanted to do your own thing?' I laughed, teasing her about this U-turn.

'I miss you,' she replied. 'And I miss all my friends. I want us all to be together again.'

While I joked with her about changing her mind, and how she just couldn't bear to be apart from me, secretly I was delighted. When we were apart it *did* feel like a bit of me was missing.

I couldn't wait for school to start again in September, when I'd have my twin at my side, where she belonged.

It was that summer when we both got our first bras – not that we needed them, because we were both still as flat as pancakes.

Every Friday, Mum would take Nana to do her weekly shopping at our local Asda and this particular week I went along too, while Nicole stayed at home because she wasn't feeling well.

Browsing the clothes section, I spied a neon pink bra hanging on the rail. I'd noticed, while getting changed for PE during the school year, that other girls in our class were starting to swap crop tops and vests for bras, and I wanted to go into second year the same as everyone else, but I also knew I didn't really need a bra yet.

Mum spotted me staring longingly at the bra and lifted it down from the rail. 'Do you like it?' she asked. 'Would you like me to get it for you?'

I nodded, thrilled at the prospect of being a bra wearer!

'Well, let's get one for you and one for Nicole, too. I can't believe my little girls are going to be wearing bras! It seems like yesterday you were both in nappies,' Mum said. 'They don't have a measuring service here but I'm going to guess you're both a double A cup.'

As soon as we got home, I rushed into our bedroom where Nicole was watching TV and showed her what Mum had bought us.

'Wow! Amazing! I feel really grown-up,' she exclaimed.

'Me too!' I agreed excitedly.

That night we chucked out all our old crop tops and vests. Realising we only had one pink bra each to wear now, Mum had to go back to the supermarket the next day to buy more to restock our now-empty underwear drawers. And for the rest of the summer we both insisted on wearing vest tops at every opportunity to show off our bra straps and let everyone know just how grown-up we were.

When September came around again, this time Nicole and I walked through the school gates together in matching uniforms. We had all the same classes, and first on our timetable that morning was Geography.

'Come on, we're going to be late,' I said, running up the stairs to the school's second floor.

Taking our seats beside one another, Nicole turned to me. 'Why are people staring at me?' she hissed. 'I just heard some guy ask the girl beside him if I was "the sick girl". Did you tell everyone I had CF?'

'Err … I might have mentioned it in a speech I did last year. I told everyone you were my hero …'

Nicole looked at me in surprise, her eyes filling with tears. 'I'm your hero? Really?'

'Of course you are! How can you not already know that?' I replied.

Reaching across the desk, Nicole squeezed my hand tight. 'And you're mine, sis.'

We were 13 when we went on a family holiday to Blackpool, staying at a small hotel beside the famous Pleasure Beach.

A foreign holiday was out of the question. Not only would it have been too expensive for us as a family, but it was unlikely that Nicole would have got travel insurance, and Mum and Dad just couldn't take the chance she'd not get sick abroad.

It was still a big undertaking to take Nicole away and Mum spent days before making sure she had enough shakes – Nicole's doctors had agreed she could have a few days off her artificial feeding if Mum gave her protein shakes instead – and medicine, and researching the nearest hospital in Blackpool just in case Nicole took a bad turn while we were away.

None of us were daredevils when it came to the rides – even Nicole, who usually was scared of nothing. But we made a pact that we'd go on at least one massive rollercoaster before the end of the holiday.

On the second to last day, we spotted one that was not only huge with lots of loops, but also sped through a big pool of water at the end, soaking everyone in the carriages.

'That's the one,' Gary said. 'Come on, it's now or never. We go home tomorrow.'

He strutted off towards the queue, trying to look uncon-cerned, but I knew he was terrified – I was too! In fact, after a few moments in the queue, watching the ride dangle people upside down, hearing them scream with fear, I knew I couldn't get on it. I turned on my heel and fled back to Mum and Dad, who were waiting for us at a nearby café.

A few moments later, Gary appeared too, looking sheepish.

'Did you chicken out too?' Dad laughed. 'Where's Nicole?'

'She's still in the queue. She said I was a wimp and there was no way she was backing out,' Gary replied.

'That's my girl,' Dad said proudly, chuckling.

Fifteen minutes later, Nicole burst into the café, windswept and exhilarated. 'I can't believe you two left me!' she said. 'I had to go on with a family I didn't know. But it was amazing. I'm so glad I did it.'

'How come you're not soaking wet, Nicole?' I asked. I had noticed that everyone coming off the same ride was drenched.

'I squeezed into the middle of that family so they all got wet but I didn't!' she replied. 'Clever, huh?'

We all burst out laughing, seeing how delighted she was with herself.

As we got older, Nicole developed a really wicked sense of humour that regularly had all of us in stitches of laughter.

For Christmas in 2004, she asked for a photo printer as a present, which she could use with her digital camera. After a huge Christmas meal, Mum, Dad and I were watching TV and dozing in front of the fire while Nicole and Gary played with their presents in his room.

Suddenly, a white envelope was pushed under the living room door. I jumped up from the sofa to get it. Opening it, I burst out laughing.

'What's so funny?' Dad asked sleepily, from the sofa.

I held up the photo contained in the envelope. It showed a blindfolded Gary, lying on the floor of his bedroom, his wrists and ankles tied together with Nicole's winter scarves. Giggling, I turned the photo over and there was a message on the back: 'Bring us two bowls of Christmas pudding if you want to see your son alive again,' it read, in what looked suspiciously like Nicole's handwriting.

'She's crazy, that girl!' Mum laughed. 'I never know what prank she's going to pull next!'

Nicole was as smart as she was funny, and we both worked hard at school. While she excelled at subjects like History and English, I was better at Maths and Science.

'You're such a geek!' she'd joke as we did our homework together at night, and I had to help her yet again with her Biology homework.

'Well, you're a bookworm!' I'd laugh, pointing to the stack of novels on her bedside table.

When it suited Nicole, she'd use her cystic fibrosis to her advantage and she nearly always skived off doing PE with the rest of the class. As we trooped outside in the freezing cold and rain to do cross-country running, she'd wave us off with a cheeky smile as she stayed behind in the warm classroom.

I didn't mind, though. I adored PE and was the fastest girl in the class, happiest when I was sprinting around the track.

One day, a list was placed on the school noticeboard with the names of the fastest runners in the whole school on it. By accident, our names had been mixed up and instead of mine, Nicole's was at the top.

'Look!' she screeched, bent double with laughter. 'I'm the speediest girl in the school!' She dined out on that for weeks, even getting a copy of the list to pin up in her bedroom.

It would have been so easy for Nicole to have felt resentful that she wasn't fit and healthy like me, but if it did bother her she never showed it, instead becoming my biggest supporter when I ran in races, cheering me on from the sidelines when she was well enough.

I loved sports so much in fact that I wanted to be a PE teacher when I grew up. Nicole's ambitions changed from day to day, but always involved animals: one day she wanted to be a veterinary nurse; the next a zookeeper or a dog groomer.

'When we've both got our careers, we'll rent a gorgeous flat in town together, Nicole,' I said one afternoon, as we did our homework in her hospital room. 'And go out shopping every weekend for clothes. Won't we, Mum?' I called over to Mum, who was hanging up Nicole's school uniform on a hanger ready for the next morning.

'Don't wish your lives away, girls. Just enjoy the here and now,' she replied.

Nicole didn't hear and carried on chatting about maybe opening up her own pet shop, but I was puzzled. It wasn't the first time Mum, and Dad as well, had been reluctant to talk about the future.

But why?

When we were younger, all Nicole really missed out on when she was in hospital was playing out in the street. But once we became teenagers, she started to miss out on more and more of normal teenage life.

And I began to learn what it was like to feel torn between my sister and my own life.

It felt like the more I was growing up and being allowed to be a bit more independent, Nicole wasn't. Even though it didn't seem like she was getting any sicker, it was as if her life was stalling just as mine was moving forward.

We were in a tight-knit group of friends at school and almost every weekend we'd both be invited to a sleepover at someone's house. But Nicole could never go. She had so many tablets, her nebuliser, her feeding machine and pouches of milk that it would have been a military operation to move her, even for one night, to someone else's house.

'You go, Melissa,' she'd say. 'I really don't mind.'

But the odd time I did, I spent the whole evening missing her and wishing she could be there watching DVDs and gossiping about the boys at school too.

During Nicole's two-week stints in hospital, although she was allowed out for school, often she had to stay in for the whole weekend, depending on what treatment the doctors wanted to give her. So, as well as spending most week nights after school there with her, I would go at weekends too.

There's not a lot to do in hospital, so we had to make our own fun. Nicole loved to make up quizzes and we would do them, testing our knowledge of pop music, sport and general trivia. We loved to watch movies, and Nicole was a huge Disney fan.

One rainy Saturday, Dad took me up to the hospital for the afternoon, to be with Nicole.

'Let's watch *The Lion King*,' she suggested. 'We haven't had it on in ages.'

Lying side by side on her hospital bed, we watched and sang along to Elton John's 'Circle of Life', our favourite song from the movie. As we sang, a nurse walked into Nicole's room to check the IV drip of antibiotics that was in her arm. Seeing us snuggled up together on the bed she stopped dead, and I could see she was trying not to cry.

'You look like two wee angels lying there,' she said, her voice choked with emotion.

At the time I didn't really understand why she'd got so upset at the sight of us but, looking back, I think how innocent and happy we must have looked, just enjoying being together; forgetting, as we sang along to the music, why we were both in a hospital on a Saturday when we should have been out in the world, living our life together.

Soon after that, we moved to another three-bedroom house in the same area.

When Mum and Dad had announced we were moving a few months before, they'd also suggested Nicole and I move into separate bedrooms for the first time in our life.

'Why?' I asked, reluctant to be apart from my sister.

'Wouldn't you both like to have your own space now you're getting a bit older?' Mum asked. 'And we think it might be better for Nicole not to be sharing a room, especially when you have a cold or a sickness bug, as then there's less chance of giving it to her.'

Nicole and I looked at one another, neither of us convinced by this plan.

'Where will you and Dad sleep?' Nicole asked. 'It's only a three-bedroom house.'

'We're going to have a sofa bed in the living room,' Mum replied. 'We'll be fine in there, and we want you kids to have your own rooms now you're all becoming teenagers. A four-bedroom house would be the perfect solution, but we just can't afford it, unfortunately.'

I felt guilty that Mum and Dad were giving up their room so we could have one each and didn't want to seem ungrateful, so I said nothing. But I wasn't keen on sleeping alone, without Nicole; it was bad enough having to do it when she was in hospital.

At first it was a novelty, and I quite liked being able to spread out all my belongings, read or watch TV as late as I wanted without disturbing Nicole, and I did feel more grown-up having my own bedroom. But, after a few weeks, I began to miss our late-night chats and knowing she was there in the bed next to me if I woke after a bad dream.

We started sneaking into one another's rooms after Mum and Dad had gone to sleep, sharing a bed.

When Mum found out she just laughed: 'Whatever makes you happy, girls!' she said, smiling at us. 'Who am I to stand in the way of my inseparable twinnies?'

We kept our separate rooms, using them to do our home-work, keep our clothes in and, of course, store Nicole's medical equipment. But, most nights, we'd share a bed in one or other room.

We might have been teenagers but we still loved cuddling up, just like when we were little girls.

Chapter Four

'Nicole, what's wrong?' I asked, running from the bedroom door to hug my sister, who was lying on her bed crying hysterically. 'What's happened? Tell me …' I said, wiping away the tears that were falling down her face.

'It's Gaynor,' she sobbed. 'She's died.'

For a moment I couldn't breathe. Nicole's words knocked the wind out of me. 'She's d-d-dead?' I stuttered. 'But she's only 13!'

'I know, but she's gone,' Nicole wailed, burying her face in my shoulder as we hugged one another tightly.

Gaynor was one of Nicole's hospital friends – part of her CF gang who all hung out together in Yorkhill when they were admitted for treatment and maintenance.

'Our other friend, Holly, just messaged me on Facebook to tell me,' Nicole went on, once she'd finally stopped crying. 'She got an infection and her lungs were too damaged – she couldn't fight it and she died yesterday.'

I could hardly take it in. How could a 13-year-old girl die and doctors not be able to save her?

I knew by then that cystic fibrosis was a serious illness but this was different. This was a wake-up call that it could kill my sister – something Mum and Dad had never admitted to either of us. I realised then that until that moment, I'd just subconsciously trusted that with all the doctors looking after her, and her weeks spent in hospital, one day someone would find a way of making Nicole better.

It simply hadn't crossed my mind that she could die.

I knew from the shell-shocked look on Nicole's face that it hadn't crossed hers either. Like me, she had just put her trust in the doctors who cared for her.

In that moment, it felt like the protective bubble created by our parents and her doctors around us both had burst. The very idea of my life without Nicole in it made me feel physically sick as I rocked her gently, feeling her body shake with heaving sobs.

For days afterwards, Nicole barely spoke a word; she was like a shadow of her former self, at school and at home.

Everyone thought she was grieving for her friend, which she was – but I knew there was also more to it than that. Gaynor's death had hit her like a sledgehammer, and a seed had been planted in her head.

My twin's intuition told me she was wondering if she was going to die, too. And that if she was, what was the point in living a life dictated by medicines, physio and hospital stays?

Was it all just a waste of time?

Just like when we were children, it was Nicole who took the lead when it came to being typical teenagers.

Not long after Gaynor died, when Nicole was 14, she got her first boyfriend. I was so relieved to see her happy and smiling again after weeks of being so quiet and unhappy at the loss of her friend. Craig was the same age as Nicole and lived just round the corner. My sister had seen him walking past our house a few times and had been desperate to find out who the 'new boy' was, so I knew she fancied him.

One day, we were all hanging out in the street and he was there. They got chatting and before I knew it, they were insepa-rable. I wasn't remotely interested in boys – too busy with my dancing, and competing in athletics at school – but Nicole was much more confident and flirtatious than me, and loved being the first of our group of friends to have a proper boyfriend. She always wanted to be 'grown-up', and I think having a boyfriend made her feel very mature. Perhaps, too, subconsciously, she knew she should grab opportunities when she could. Having cystic fibrosis made her determined not to waste time or wait for something she wanted – she was always impatient to live life to the full, including being in love.

Craig quite simply worshipped the ground Nicole walked on. He came to our house every day after school and they would spend hours just watching TV, playing board games and talking. She was definitely the boss in their relationship, as Craig was very quiet and painfully shy. They say opposites attract and it was definitely true of them.

Nicole told me that what she loved most about Craig was that he accepted her for who she was, and saw past the cystic fibrosis to the girl underneath. 'He doesn't care if I cough up phlegm or if he has to visit me in hospital instead of going on a date like he would with a "normal" girl,' she confided one evening. 'He even helps with my physio. There's not many boys our age who are that mature and lovely. He knows that cystic fibrosis is a part of who I am, unfortunately, but he accepts that and loves me anyway.'

The Christmas we were 15, Mum and Dad bought Nicole a Westie puppy called LouLou. Craig and Nicole treated the pup like their baby, cuddling her on the sofa and taking her for short strolls around the block because Nicole couldn't walk too far.

When Nicole had to stay in hospital, Craig would visit every day. He saved his pocket money to buy her bunches of flowers, and for her birthday bought her four teddy bears, which she named John, Paul, George and Ringo because she loved The Beatles. He doted on her: whatever Nicole wanted, Craig would do, and I teased her about having him under the thumb.

I was so happy for her. Having a boyfriend was a taste of normal teenage life for Nicole, and helped her feel more like everyone else. And, far from feeling jealous of their closeness, I was pleased she had someone else apart from me to spend time with when she was stuck in the house or hospital.

Later that year, Nicole was diagnosed with a type of diabetes only suffered by people with cystic fibrosis. The disease affects the pancreas as well as the lungs, and means it can't produce enough insulin to control blood-sugar levels.

For as long as I could remember, Nicole had been tested for it regularly because of this known link between the two conditions, so when she was diagnosed it wasn't too much of a shock. And, as with so much that was thrown at her, Nicole took it in her stride.

Every day she had to check her blood-sugar levels by pricking her finger with a fine needle and placing a drop of her blood on a test strip. Then she'd have to inject herself with insulin, plunging a sharp needle into her tummy or thighs.

'You're so brave, Nicole,' I said, watching her as we got ready for school one morning.

'Yes, it's just as well I'm not a scaredy cat when it comes to needles, like you, isn't it?' she laughed. 'I'm like a pincushion! I've had so many needles in me over the years, it doesn't faze me.'

What Nicole found a lot harder, though, was controlling her diet. She had a sweet tooth and after years of being encouraged to eat high-calorie foods – because cystic fibrosis meant it was incredibly hard to keep her body at a healthy weight – now her diet was more restricted.

One afternoon I arrived home from my dancing class to find all hell had broken loose in Nicole's bedroom.

'What are you playing at?' Mum was shouting angrily. 'Are you crazy? Do you know how bad all this is for you? You could end up in a diabetic coma!'

'You shouldn't have been snooping in my wardrobe!' Nicole shouted back. 'It's none of your business, Mum.'

I walked into the room to find them eyeballing one another across a massive pile of packets of sweets, chocolate bars and fizzy drinks lying strewn across Nicole's bed.

'I've found her secret stash,' Mum said, turning to me and pointing at the confectionary on the bed. Gathering it up in her arms, she looked at my sister. 'You're 15 now, Nicole. You have to grow up and realise you need to take care of your body.'

Nicole looked at me and rolled her eyes before flopping down on the bed as Mum stomped out of the room, slamming the door in anger behind her.

'I'm sick of being treated like a baby. Here … at hospital – I never get to do what *I* want,' Nicole shouted after her.

For a few days afterwards, you could have cut the atmosphere in our house with a knife. Nicole and Mum were both seething, and Gary and I felt very uncomfortable stuck between them. To an outsider, it might have just seemed like a petty row over some sweets, but I knew it symbolised much more than that. Nicole was becoming an adult, trying to assert herself and take control of her own body, albeit in a really irresponsible way on this occasion. Mum, meanwhile, was losing control over her little girl and was terrified that if she wasn't able to take care of her, there could be serious consequences.

Although things returned to normal after a few days, I wondered how long it would be before they would cross swords again about who was in charge of Nicole's care.

Yorkhill hospital was like Nicole's second home, and mine. We knew every inch of it, every member of staff, and her room there was as familiar to us as her bedroom at home. But, after turning 15, Nicole was told she had to move to a new hospital called Gartnavel General, in the west of the city.

'Why can't I stay at Yorkhill?' she asked Mum, who'd broken the news over dinner.

'Well, even though you'll always be my baby, the doctors say you're an adult patient now, and Yorkhill is just for children. So they can't look after you there any more,' Mum replied.

'Will I still have to go in every two months for a fortnight?' Nicole asked.

'No, you won't. They will only admit you when you're poorly. I'm not happy about that, though – I like a close eye being kept on you, but that's just the way it is.'

A massive smile broke out across Nicole's face. 'That's brilliant!' she squealed, punching the air in delight.

But Nicole's happiness at transferring hospitals didn't last long. Within a few weeks, she had a bad chest infection and was admitted to Gartnavel. It was a massive shock for her, and me. Because it was a children's hospital, Yorkhill had been painted in bright, cheery colours with murals on the walls and toys everywhere to distract its young patients from the fact they were poorly. Gartnavel, by comparison, was dreary and dull, with that horrible hospital smell which sticks to your clothes and skin for days afterwards. It was also very quiet, and there was a depressing atmosphere I dreaded – it gave me goosebumps.

'I hate it here,' Nicole whispered to me as I sat by her bedside, flicking through our favourite celebrity magazines.

Looking around I didn't blame her. She was on the respiratory ward, and was the youngest patient by about 40 years.

'An old lady died in the bed next to me last night,' she said softly. 'I was scared. I wanted you here, La La.'

I shuddered at the thought of my sister all alone in a ward, surrounded by people who were dying. It was so unfair – she was just 15 years old. She should have been at school, or out with me and our friends, not stuck on a hospital ward yet again.

Added to this, now that Nicole was classed as an adult patient, doctors and nurses began to be much more open with her about her cystic fibrosis. At Yorkhill, it had been Mum and Dad they spoke to about her treatment and how her health was, but at Gartnavel they came straight to her.

Slowly, Nicole started to learn what having cystic fibrosis really meant, after years of being cocooned from the harsh reality of the disease. She began to sit up late at night, researching the disease on her laptop, then bombarding the doctors with questions at her regular appointments.

The internet told her everything. There was no hiding the grim truth from her any more.

She was 16 when she first began to talk about getting a lung transplant. 'I've been reading about it online. It would make me so much better, Melissa – can you imagine that? I could be a normal person for the first time ever,' she said, her face lit up with hope.

The following day she returned from a check-up at hospital, full of information.

'When we were born, the life expectancy of someone born with CF was only about 20. But since then the treatment has improved, and my doctor says now it's around 40. But if I got a lung transplant I could live as long as you!' She beamed at me. 'So I'm going to need a lung transplant. I have to be put on a special list then wait until someone dies who is the right match for me. Their healthy lungs will be given to me, and my useless ones will be chucked in the bin. So I don't want you to worry about me, OK? I'll get one, I'm sure of it.'

Listening to her, it all sounded so straightforward, and I could see she had utter faith she would get a transplant. Nicole had always been the glass-half-full twin – I was the glass-half-empty one – and this was no different. I just didn't share her confidence, and a dark feeling I'd never had before washed over me. Surely there was a massive waiting list, and what were the chances someone would die who was the perfect match for her? Typically, Nicole had breezed over the part about her life expectancy without a transplant, focusing on the positive news.

But what if a match wasn't found in time?

I kept my doubts to myself; I knew it wouldn't help her if I shared them, but I fretted that while she believed a cure was in sight, maybe it just wasn't that simple.

While Nicole *was* really positive about the prospect of a lung transplant, what she learned about her disease was often frightening. Her way of coping with it was to tell me in a casual way, dropping it into conversation, as if it was no big deal.

One evening at home, we were sitting together watching the TV programme *One Born Every Minute*. As the new mother cradled her baby, Nicole turned to me. 'When you have babies, Melissa, I'll be the best auntie ever. I'll spoil them rotten,' she said.

'And I'll do the same for your kids,' I replied.

'Oh, didn't I tell you?' she said casually, looking straight ahead at the TV to avoid eye contact with me. 'I won't be able to have children.'

I almost spilt my cup of tea all over the sofa. 'When did you find this out?' I spluttered. 'How do you feel about it?'

'It's just one of those things, isn't it?' she replied nonchalantly. 'I read about it online. Because my CF is so severe and I'm so slight, pregnancy would put too much strain on my body and my lungs, and make my cystic fibrosis worse.' She picked at a stray thread on the cuff of her top. 'Even after a transplant, getting pregnant could cause my body to reject the new lungs. So it's just not going to be something I can even contemplate. I'm OK about it.'

'Have you told Craig about this?' I asked, wondering what her boyfriend of two years would think about the fact that if they stayed together, he'd never be a father.

'Of course, and he's fine with it. I mean, we're only 16, so having kids probably isn't something he's thought much about anyway, but he told me I'm what's important to him. Anything else, we can deal with together.' She turned to look at me then. 'Maybe you could be my surrogate and have one for me!' she laughed, but it was forced.

I could tell she didn't want to talk about it anymore but I didn't believe for a second she wasn't bothered by what she had learned. I knew my sister better than anyone and she adored children. When we were small, her half of our room had been cluttered with dolls and Barbies that she fussed over, and she was always the first to coo into a pram at a new baby. But I also knew that this was her way of coping with what she was discovering about her disease: if she made out to me, and other people, that it wasn't scary, then she could try to convince herself of that.

But she couldn't fool me.

I knew she was hurting, and I felt so helpless.

Chapter Five

Nicole and I always did as much as we possibly could together. It just always felt better that way. So when an advert appeared in the window of an empty shop unit near our house in 2007, announcing a branch of Domino's was opening and staff were needed, we immediately decided to apply for part-time jobs. We were 16 and ready to have some money of our own, instead of just pocket money from Mum and Dad.

The following week, we were both told to come in for an interview after school, one after the other.

I went in first, then waited outside for Nicole to do her interview.

'So, what did you say?' she asked, as we walked the short distance home, Nicole having to stop occasionally to cough into a hanky.

'I said I'm hardworking, tidy and punctual,' I answered. 'I couldn't really say much more because I've never had a job before. What did you say?'

'I told them my ambition is to be a chef, I'm top of my class in Home Economics and I do all the cooking at home. In fact, pizzas are my speciality!' she replied with a cheeky smile and a glint in her eye.

'You fibber! None of that's true – you don't even do Home Ec!'

'I know, but they won't know that and I *really* want a part-time job.'

The following day we were telephoned and told we'd each got a job, working on a Friday and Saturday evening. We were ecstatic. Not only was it our first job, but we'd be doing it together.

For the next six months we made pizzas, took orders by telephone and cleaned up. We loved working together and, typically, Nicole bossed everyone around even though the rest of the staff were older than us.

'Your sister is a hoot,' one of the delivery guys said to me laughing, as we locked up one night. 'She makes me laugh so much. I'd never have known she was ill if she hadn't told me.'

Not for the first time I felt proud that, despite her illness, Nicole was not only working but so popular with all our colleagues.

'I know,' I said to him. 'She's pretty special.'

We couldn't wait to get our pay every week, feeling so grown-up to have our own money for the first time. I was fashion-obsessed and all of mine went straight on clothes, my wardrobe bursting with the latest styles from my favourite shops like New Look and Oasis. Nicole spent hers on DVDs and trips to the cinema because she'd become such a movie buff – a side effect, she said, of years spent in hospital with nothing to do but watch films.

We were 16 when our beloved Nana died. Apart from when Nicole's childhood friend, Gaynor, had passed away, it was the first time we'd ever experienced a death, especially of someone we loved so much.

Nana was 85 and just slipped away in her sleep, at our house. She'd come to stay for a few nights because she wasn't feeling well, and had died while she was having a nap, my mum and Katrina at her side.

I was watching TV in the living room with Nicole and Gary when Katrina came into the room, ashen-faced. 'She's gone,' she said. 'She's not breathing ...' Nicole and I sat, completely stunned, trying to take in the fact our Nana had just died when, only an hour before, we'd brought her a cup of tea in bed and chatted to her as she'd drifted off to sleep.

As Katrina hugged us both, Gary stood up and walked out of the house, not returning until late that night. That was just the way he dealt with emotional situations – he backed away from them. He found it easier to grieve privately and bottle up his feelings rather than share them, and I understood that was just how he was.

Almost worse than losing Nana was seeing the effect her death had on Mum. She was inconsolable – it was like a light had gone out in her eyes for months afterwards. All our lives she had been the strong one of the family, holding us all together during the hardest of times. To see her so broken by grief was frightening and I didn't like it. I realised how much I relied on Mum's stoicism ... how much we all did.

Neither Nicole nor I wanted to go to university and so in 2008, we both left school after our fifth year.

Leaving school is such a big milestone for everyone. It's the end of your childhood in one way, and the start of your life as an adult. But, walking out of the school gates together for the last time, I had no idea that it was a different sort of milestone for Nicole and me: from that moment, life would start to pull us in very different directions, threatening the closeness we'd had and the bond we'd shared for 16 years.

Within a few weeks of leaving school, I landed a job as a supervisor at a luxury handbag shop at Silverburn Shopping Centre on the outskirts of Glasgow. I loved it. The hours were long and I was always rushed off my feet, but I thrived on the thrill of earning a proper salary for the first time, and because most of my friends were still at school or at college, I felt really grown-up by comparison.

While I went straight from school to full-time work, Nicole had decided to go to Reid Kerr College in Paisley, to study to become a medical secretary. She'd decided she wanted a career in the NHS so she could give a little bit back after her years of treatment. But a role in a hospital was out of the question: her cystic fibrosis meant she was too much at risk of picking up bugs and infections that could have left her seriously affected. And so she had decided to go for an administrative job, working as a medical secretary.

Within a few weeks, it became obvious how different our lives were becoming. I was out all day working, I had my own money, new friends and came home every day buzzing about the sophisticated women I'd served that day, and the gorgeous shop I was in charge of. And, four nights a week, I only came home to get changed before going straight out again, to bars and clubs in town with my new work friends – I had no problem fooling the bouncers that I was 18.

I was still a teenager but I felt very grown-up, excited to be part of the adult world of work and loving my new social life. Caught up in the excitement of my new life, I didn't think as much as I should have about Nicole.

Her life was a lot less exciting. Monday to Friday she went to college, but often she wasn't well enough and had to miss her classes, which left her feeling stressed and unhappy. In the evenings she stayed in because she didn't have any money.

She was still going out with Craig, and he was as devoted as ever, but he was working too and Nicole would encourage him to see his friends as well as her, not wanting him to miss out on a social life because of her.

'I'll lend you some money,' I offered one Friday night, as I was getting ready to go out and she was sitting miserably on the bed, watching me put on my make-up.

'Thanks, sis, but there's no point. I wouldn't get in anywhere, anyway.'

It was true. Nicole was small and slight, and looked closer to 13 than 17. Her posture was bad because of the strain her constant coughing put on her back and chest muscles, meaning she hunched over, making her look even smaller. Wheezy and breathless, she regularly had coughing fits which could last for several minutes and were often so violent she would be physically sick from the sheer force of coughing. No – while I breezed past bouncers at the doors of pubs and clubs, Nicole would never have got in, even if she'd been well enough to leave the house, which increasingly she wasn't.

I started to feel torn. Part of me loved my new life and wanted to embrace it, but another part of me felt guilty that Nicole couldn't share it with me.

'Maybe I should cancel my plans and stay in with Nicole,' I whispered to Mum in the kitchen, out of earshot of my sister, who was watching TV in the living room next door.

'Melissa, you can't stop being who you are because Nicole is ill,' she replied. 'You have to live your own life, not put it on hold. What good would that do? Nothing. Your sister understands that. Now go out and enjoy yourself.'

But, out that night in a local bar, surrounded by my friends, I just couldn't enjoy myself, thinking of Nicole stuck at home.

'Here's your drink,' a colleague shouted over the loud dance music playing in the bar.

Sipping my cocktail and listening to everyone laugh and chat around me, I did my best not to think about my sister. Mum was right: not living my life wasn't going to make her better but, as one of her favourite songs started to play and I watched everyone dancing away, I felt angry for her. Why did she have to be sick and miss out on so much? It was so unfair. And why did I have to feel guilty about just trying to live a normal life? No one seemed to realise how hard it was for me as well.

Desperate to feel normal, Nicole started looking for part-time work while she was at college. First she went to work in a local fish factory, cleaning out the tanks. But it was cold, messy work and she was exhausted when she came home after every shift.

When she came down with a serious chest infection, Mum put her foot down. 'I know you want to work and earn some money of your own, but you're not cut out for a job like this,' she said, as Nicole lay pale and coughing on her bed. 'If you don't call your boss and resign, I'll do it for you.'

Next, Nicole tried working as a sales assistant in a local sari shop. We teased her a lot about how she stood out like a sore thumb with her pale skin and red hair among all the glamorous Asian customers who shopped there. But again, after just a couple of weeks, she was exhausted and sick after being on her feet for hours at a time.

'No job is worth your health, Nicole,' I said to her the day she handed in her notice. 'You've done the right thing.'

I knew she was desperate to be normal: to have a job, some money, a grown-up life like me and everyone else. But it was all just too much for her.

'I can do it up here,' she sighed, pointing to her head. 'But it's my body that keeps letting me down. It's so frustrating.'

Not long after that, Nicole had to drop out of college. She was missing too many classes through illness to keep up with the course.

As her life came to a grinding halt, Nicole became more and more withdrawn, spending hours alone in her room. She didn't want to see anyone, from friends to Craig, lost in her sadness at the limbo her life had become, thanks to her illness.

I knew she was unhappy but I didn't know what to do to help. And, slowly, I became the target of her unhappiness.

I never knew what sort of mood Nicole would be in when I got home from work: one day, she was my best friend; the next she was furious with me just for using her hair straighteners. The smallest thing could spark her temper and I found myself walking on eggshells around her.

I wasn't stupid; I knew why I was bearing the brunt of her bad moods. I had everything she wanted: a job, a social life and, most of all, good health. She had none of that; instead, her life was one of medicine, illness and dead ends.

One Friday evening I came home from work, tired, and looking forward to a night on the sofa with a Chinese takeaway.

'Is that my cardigan you're wearing?' Nicole snapped at me the moment I walked through the front door. 'You never asked if you could borrow it.'

'Sorry, I was in a rush this morning and just grabbed it on my way out to work,' I replied, shocked at the sharp tone of her voice.

'You're a selfish cow!' she screamed at me, her face contorted with rage. 'How dare you take my things without asking! It's not my problem you spend all your money on going out and can't afford new clothes. You've no right to nick mine. I hate you!'

I couldn't believe she could say such cruel things to me. 'You've gone too far this time, Nicole,' I said, shaking with anger. 'I know you're unhappy, I know you're jealous of me ... but that's not my fault. Stop blaming me all the time! You know I would swap places with you if I could.'

Turning around, I walked out of the house, slamming the front door. As I stumbled down the path, unable to see through my tears, I could hear Nicole crying in the house.

'I can't handle this,' I heard Mum shout at her. 'What has happened to you both?'

I walked for twenty minutes to our cousin Katrina's home, where I spent the night, needing some space and time to calm down.

Katrina listened to me talk for hours, angry with Nicole at first for being so mean to me, then upset that in getting on with my life I was making her so unhappy.

'She's just lashing out in frustration and, unfortunately, sometimes we punish the people we're closest to when we're feeling like that,' Katrina said wisely. 'I know it's not easy for you, but you just need to be patient and not let it get to you. I'm sure this bad patch she's going through will pass soon, and then you'll be back to being best friends again.'

The next day I went home feeling nervous, not sure of the reception I was going to get.

'I'm sorry, Melissa,' Nicole said quietly, as soon as I walked through the door. 'I was completely out of order.'

'It's OK. I understand,' I replied, as we hugged tightly.

But, inside, I was still shocked she had attacked me so viciously. It was an eye-opener. I realised now just how hard it was for Nicole to watch me live the life she was desperate to have.

For the next few weeks we tiptoed around one another, being unusually polite, before eventually things returned to normal. From then on, though, it didn't matter how many people told me I shouldn't put my life on hold; I realised I needed to make more time for my sister. And if that meant making sacrifices in my own life then so be it. Her happiness was worth every one of them.

Just before we turned 17, Nicole announced she was going away for a weekend with Craig.

Her mood was more upbeat because her health had stabilised a bit, and she'd stopped shutting herself away in her room, night after night.

I laughed when she told me they were going to Alton Towers, by themselves. 'Mum and Dad will never in a million years let you go off for a weekend to a hotel by yourselves. You know how strict they are when it comes to boys – even Craig, who's like part of the family. You're crazy if you think they'll agree to it.'

'We'll see …' said Nicole, with that look in her eyes that I knew meant she was determined to get her own way on this.

The next day she came prancing into my room, a huge smile on her face. 'I'm off to Alton Towers with Craig next weekend. Told you so!' she said cheekily. 'Mum and Dad have said yes.'

I couldn't believe it, knowing they would never have let me do anything like that.

'She has so little fun in her life, we didn't want to stand in her way,' Mum explained, when I asked her about it later. 'She deserves a bit of freedom and independence – she has so little of it normally.'

I could see where Mum was coming from, and she was right. Nicole had so few opportunities to enjoy herself, she shouldn't have to miss out on any more than she already did.

Waving her and Craig off the following weekend, I could see that for once she felt like the grown-up twin, and I was glad for her.

*

In October 2009, Nicole and I turned 18.

For the first time in ages Nicole's health was stable, and we decided to throw a huge party to celebrate our birthday. We'd always had a joint bash every year, but this time we were determined to really push the boat out, hiring the function room of a local sports club for the night and decorating it with balloons and 'Happy 18th Birthday' banners.

It was Nicole who decided we should make it a fancy-dress party.

'It's nearly Halloween, and it'll be fun to see everyone dressed up,' she said, as we drew up our guest list. 'I'm going to go as Poison Ivy from the Batman films. She's got red hair and pale skin, just like me!'

I decided to continue her Batman theme and dress up as The Riddler, while Katrina went as Batgirl and her partner Peter was Robin. Craig was there too, of course, dressed as Zorro. Ever the devoted boyfriend, he made sure Nicole always had a drink in her hand, and when they weren't slow-dancing together he watched her dancing with our friends, a soppy expression on his face.

Over 120 people were at the party and the dancefloor was packed with people dressed up in amazing costumes. Our cousins Dianne and Christine were nuns; our cousin John was Neo from *The Matrix* in a black suit and sunglasses; and although our half-sister Laura couldn't make it, Kelly had flown up for the night to celebrate with us.

From the outside it probably looked like your average eighteenth birthday: there was a buffet for which Mum had made all the food, a huge cake with 'Happy 18th Birthday Nicole and Melissa' iced on it, and a DJ who played cheesy tunes all night. But there was a special atmosphere too – a feeling of hope in the air shared by all of us that this milestone, marking Nicole's and my transition into adulthood, was going to be a positive one. That her adult years were going to be so much better than her childhood had been.

'Where's Nicole?' I asked Mum halfway through the night, unable to find my sister among the hordes of party-goers.

'There she is.' Mum pointed to the middle of the dancefloor.

Nicole was dancing with a group of friends, a massive smile on her face as she sang along with the music. The glitterball hanging above her cast little twinkling lights all over her face, and she looked so incredibly happy I felt a lump in my throat.

'I wish she could always be so happy,' I murmured to Mum, fighting back tears.

'I know, me too. I can't believe my wee baby girls are 18 years old. Where has that time gone?' Mum replied. 'Let's hope the years ahead are happier ones for her, and all of us.'

'Come on, Melissa! Come and dance,' Nicole shouted over the music, gesturing for me to join her.

We danced all night, surrounded by all the people we loved the most, but the only person who really mattered to me was Nicole as she twirled around under the glittering lights.

Chapter Six

After we turned 18, I decided I wanted to go back to college.

After leaving school at just 16, I realised I wanted more education and enrolled on an Access To Science course at a local college. After years of spending time in hospital with Nicole, watching the staff do their jobs, I had started to contemplate a career in nursing. I wasn't sure yet, however, but I reckoned that this course would help me if I wanted to go down that road.

As part of the course, we were taught about cystic fibrosis. For the first time I found I was learning first-hand about the disease, instead of through Nicole, or Mum and Dad.

So much of what I learned was frightening. Two people in the UK die from CF every week. I was horrified when I read that sufferers end up gasping for breath as they basically drown in the mucus clogging their lungs. Without enough oxygen, their organs pack up and they pass away.

I couldn't even think about my sister suffering such a slow and horrible death, and immediately stopped reading about the worst-case scenario, focusing instead on the cases of people who had lived for many years with the disease, or others who got a lung transplant and a new lease of life.

The problem was, I didn't know which of those people Nicole was going to be: one of the tragedies, or one of the inspiring cases.

I remembered that dark feeling I'd had when Nicole had first started talking about getting a transplant two years before; my sense of foreboding that it just wasn't as simple as she believed. It was still there, buried in the back of my mind – that fear of losing my sister to this horrible disease. I just couldn't explain it to myself – why I felt so negative about the future – but no matter how hard I tried, I couldn't shake my pessimism every time someone talked about Nicole getting a transplant.

I hoped desperately I was wrong, and that this wasn't twin intuition.

Nicole broke up with Craig not long after our eighteenth birthday party.

Nothing dramatic happened – things just fizzled out between them like in lots of teenage relationships, but I knew that, for Nicole, becoming single again was a much bigger deal than for other girls her age. She knew it wouldn't be as easy for her to meet someone else who was prepared to take on all the problems that came with her having cystic fibrosis. I knew she wanted to find that right person, but was conscious he was going to have to be as special as Craig to cope with having a girlfriend, and maybe wife, with such a serious illness and all its repercussions – like not being able to have children.

At first her break-up with Craig was messy in a childish way. I think they were both hurting; him about being left by her, and her at falling out of love with someone who, in so many ways, was so perfect for her. They stopped speaking and played pranks on each other: she posted an ad on Gumtree advertising tickets for a sold-out Frankie Boyle show, and put Craig's phone number on it so that he was plagued with nuisance calls; in revenge, he ordered 20 pizzas to be delivered to our house, in Nicole's name. Within a few weeks, though, they had made up and became good friends. I felt relieved that even if he wasn't her boyfriend, Craig was still a part of Nicole's life.

It was around this time that Nicole's quality of life really began to suffer, as her health deteriorated further. Unable to go to college or work, she was practically housebound by now. No job, no more education, no relationship and fewer and fewer friends as people got caught up in their own lives.

Nicole so hated to be pitied that I never told her just how much it hurt me to see her have to live a half-life like this. In the months since she'd danced the night away at our joint birthday party, her heath had steadily declined and now she was like someone who permanently had bad flu. She was breathless and wheezing, with a hacking cough, and always exhausted. Some days she couldn't get out of bed, she was so tired.

I hated seeing her like this – as if she was an old woman, not a teenager.

Every time she had a coughing fit, or was too weak to even sit at the table for a family meal, the statistics I'd read about cystic fibrosis deaths flashed through my mind. Everyone could see she was getting sicker. When was this transplant she had so much faith in going to happen?

Doctors had told Nicole that to be put on the list for a transplant, there was a very fine line between being sick enough to warrant being considered for a transplant but not too sick to survive the operation. The window when someone was suitable for transplant was a very short one, they explained.

Nicole was frustrated and impatient. She knew she was getting more and more ill and wanted to be on the list as soon as possible, but there was nothing she could do but wait and hope it would be soon.

After we'd turned 18, Nicole had insisted it was time she took responsibility for her treatment: 'I'm an adult now, Mum. I can look after myself and you need a break from caring for me,' she'd told our mum.

I could tell that Mum was anxious about it. For 18 years, every day of her life had revolved around Nicole's care – from giving her medicine, doing her physiotherapy, making sure she ate properly to control her diabetes to hooking her up to the feeding machine at night. Suddenly, she'd lost control and I saw how worried she was.

And she was right to be. Almost every day, she and Nicole argued about her treatment. Some days Nicole didn't take her medicine on time; on others she didn't do the breathing exercises she'd been taught at the hospital to help her lung-function.

Seeing Nicole neglect her health was torture for Mum.

Sitting around the dinner table one evening, before I knew it, an argument had started.

'Shall I give you some physio after dinner, Nicole?' Mum asked hopefully.

'No, Mum.' Nicole sighed. 'I've already told you, I'll do my breathing exercises instead. Stop nagging me.'

'Are you sure? You didn't do them last night. You're not taking care of yourself,' Mum said sharply, her patience with Nicole running out.

'Leave me alone! I'm an adult, I'll do what I want when I want, OK?' Nicole snapped, rolling her eyes.

'Don't you talk to me like that, young lady!' Mum shouted. 'I'm your mother and I'm just trying to do my best for you.'

On and on they went, until I stood up and left the table, my head hurting from the shouting.

I could see their arguments from both sides: Mum was terrified; she knew what the consequences were if Nicole didn't keep on top of her treatment. She'd get infections which would damage her lungs even further, and leave her even sicker. But for Nicole, this was the first time in her life she'd been in control of her body and she was rebelling, doing what *she* wanted for a change, not what she was told to do. It was stupid of Nicole and I didn't blame Mum for being angry, but I also knew Nicole was stubborn and the more she was pushed, the more she would dig her heels in.

I did my best to keep out of their battles. Nicole could still be very short-tempered when she was having a bad day, and I didn't want to go back to those days when she took her moods out on me.

None of us could have predicted how far Nicole would go in rebelling against her illness, however.

It was a sunny Sunday in August 2011 and I was lying on the sofa watching *Hollyoaks* after a late night, clubbing. Half asleep, I woke up with a start as Dad walked into the room, his face ashen.

'I'm taking Nicole to the hospital,' he said, searching for his car keys.

'What's wrong with her?' I asked, jumping up from the sofa. 'She seemed OK this morning.'

Dad took a long, ragged breath. 'I was lying on my bed watching TV and she came and lay beside me. She hugged me and started crying. "I love you," she said to me. "I've done something really stupid, Dad. I've taken too much insulin."'

I couldn't believe what I was hearing: Nicole had deliberately taken an overdose?

He walked out of the room and I followed him into Nicole's bedroom, where she lay crying on her bed, her face ghostly pale.

Dad scooped her up into his arms like she was a little girl and quickly walked out of the house, Mum following behind, before placing her gently in the front seat of the car.

I stood on the pavement looking at her crying in the front seat. She looked so frightened.

'Why, Nicole?' I mouthed to her. 'Why?' I was so shocked at what was happening I didn't know what else to say.

She just shrugged her shoulders and looked away until the car drove off.

Gary was at his work, at a high-street shoe shop, so I was home alone. I paced the floor, waiting for news. I phoned Mum and Dad's mobiles over and over again but both were switched off. Was this just because they were in the hospital and not allowed to use them, or had something awful happened? I didn't know, and felt like I was going crazy with worry.

Eventually, in the middle of the afternoon, Dad phoned. 'She's been in the resuscitation room because they weren't sure how much she'd taken and she could have slipped into a coma or even died.' His voice sounded hollow. 'But she's OK. The doctors want to keep her in for another couple of hours to keep an eye on her, but we should be home tonight.'

My legs went weak with relief at hearing Nicole was going to be all right. 'Can I talk to Mum?' I asked.

'She's too upset. It's been a huge shock to her ... to us both ... that Nicole would do something like this,' Dad said softly.

I felt an unexpected flash of anger as I hung up the phone. What was Nicole playing at, putting our parents through something like this when they had to cope with so much already? How could she have been so stupid and selfish, risking her life and adding more stress and worry to all our lives?

I'd calmed down a bit by the time they finally got home at 10 o'clock, all of them looking shattered and pale.

'Are you OK?' I asked Nicole.

'Is it OK if we don't talk about it tonight?' she asked. 'I'm really tired. I just want to go to sleep.'

She was so quiet and shaken up, and went straight to bed.

I lay awake all night, unable to sleep a wink. As my anger with her had subsided, and I had begun to really ask why she'd done something so dangerous, there was just one answer going around and around in my head.

This was a cry for help to tell us that she wasn't coping.

I could hear Mum and Dad, sitting up until the wee hours in the living room, talking about what had happened. And it was obvious they were thinking the same as me.

'Do you think she really meant to hurt herself?' Mum asked, her voice laden with hurt and confusion.

'I don't know, Agnes, I just don't know. But whatever is going on in her head, she's not coping. She's been so strong for so long – maybe we've expected too much of her and just assumed she can always take everything in her stride,' Dad replied sadly.

Listening to them talk, I began to cry quietly, turning my face to my pillow to muffle the sound of my sobs. They were right. Nicole had always been such a coper: whatever her illness had thrown at her, she'd always faced it head-on and got on with life as best she could. But this act revealed she wasn't as strong as we all thought she was, underneath her tough exterior.

Our family had a bad habit of sweeping things under the carpet, and the next morning, over breakfast, no one spoke about what had happened. In fact, no one spoke at all, the sound of my knife scraping butter onto my slice of toast deafening in the uncomfortable silence.

Perhaps Mum and Dad were too scared to delve any more into what was going on in Nicole's mind. It would make it too real to hear her say she'd had enough of living like this. But I had to know what had driven my sister to do such a thing.

I snuck a peek at Nicole across the table. She was lost in her own thoughts, a million miles away, and she looked pale and exhausted.

I waited until we were alone in the kitchen, clearing up the breakfast dishes. 'How do you feel?' I asked. 'Be honest with me, Nicole. I need to know what's going on.'

'I'm … I'm OK now. Yesterday was frightening, though. I didn't know what was going to happen.'

'Why did you do it?'

'I don't know … Can we just forget about it?'

I knew Nicole well enough to know when she had clammed up and didn't want to talk about something. 'Just promise me you'll never do anything like that again,' I asked, looking straight at her.

'I promise,' she replied. 'I promise.'

Soon after Nicole's overdose, I started going out with Martin, after one of my friends introduced us. A trainee electrician, he was my first serious boyfriend, and I was quickly head over heels for him.

When I first started dating him I worried that Nicole might feel pushed out; but I needn't have, because she and Martin got on like a house on fire from the day they met. It was then that I realised why I liked him so much: he was the male version of my sister. They were both witty, with a sharp sense of humour and an infectious laugh.

Both Martin and Nicole were movie buffs, and we'd ask her to the cinema any time we went, or the three of us would spend a rainy afternoon watching a stack of DVDs.

'I'm not in the way, am I?' Nicole asked me once. 'Tell me to bugger off if you want to be on your own with Martin. I won't be offended.'

But the truth was I was happiest when I was with both of them, and loved the fact they got on so well.

Martin was the only person I confided in about my fears for the future and my pessimism about Nicole's chances of getting a transplant.

He would try and reassure me: 'I understand why you're feeling like this, but you've just got to think positively, Melissa. I'm sure it's all going to work out OK.'

I felt like I was banging my head off a brick wall. Everyone else was so positive, I felt like a traitor. And always now, at the back of my mind, was the memory of Nicole's overdose and the knowledge that her ability to cope was wearing thin. I didn't know how much more she could handle. More than ever it felt like time was running out.

Imperceptibly, after the overdose something changed in the way we all treated Nicole – Mum and Dad especially. It had opened their eyes to the emotional battle she was fighting every day, alongside the physical one. The arguments about her treatment stopped, and although it was unspoken, I sensed they were more in tune with her frustrations about her life than they ever had been before.

One day I overheard Mum on the phone to a friend: 'Her life is nothing like her sister's and her friends. She's bored, she's sad … I don't blame her. What sort of life is this for a 19-year-old girl?'

Nicole, in turn, became much more diligent about her treatment, taking her medicine on time and, for a couple of months, letting Mum do her physiotherapy again. It seemed the overdose had scared her into taking care of herself.

But her new-found sensibleness wasn't to last.

Chapter Seven

Dozing off as we watched TV in bed, my mobile buzzed with a text message.

'Who's that?' Martin asked me sleepily.

'It's Nicole,' I replied. 'She says she's not feeling well. She's got a chest infection and is a bit down in the dumps. I think I'll go home and stay with her tonight.'

'OK,' replied Martin. 'You're a great sister, you know. Nicole's really lucky.'

'Don't be silly, she'd do the same for me if it was the other way around,' I said, pulling on my coat over my pyjamas.

It was May 2012 and after deciding a career in nursing wasn't right for me, I'd taken a job with an electricity company as a customer advisor. And, as Martin and my relationship had become more serious, I was spending half the week at his house and half at home.

At first it was really strange not seeing Nicole every day. I missed having my breakfast with her and seeing her when I got in from work. But she knew how much I cared about Martin and had encouraged me to spend time with him, just the two of us.

On the days I wasn't at home, Nicole and I spoke on the phone 10 times a day, usually about nothing important, but it was as if we just had to hear each other's voices every day, so close was our twin bond. It was just like when we were little girls and she was in hospital for weeks at a time: neither of us would go to bed until we'd spoken on the phone and sung our special song to one another.

Driving the 15-minute journey home through deserted roads, I felt anxious about Nicole's late-night text, but I didn't know why. I'd seen her that morning, and although she had been pale and coughing a lot, she had been no worse than she'd been lots of time before, so I hadn't felt unduly worried about her. But it was really strange she had texted me so late when she knew I was staying at Martin's.

I hoped it was nothing more serious than her feeling a bit fed up and wanting some cheering up. She'd had one chest infection after the other in the past few months, and what hadn't helped was that she'd been lax about staying on top of her treatment again.

After the insulin overdose the summer before, Nicole had been really diligent about having physio, doing her breathing exercises and taking her medicines but, lately, she'd let things slide again. I understood it was hard for her to see the benefit in spending the time taking care of herself when it never made her any better, but it frustrated me so much when her health suffered even more because of it.

Unlocking the front door, I went straight to Nicole's room, where she was propped up in bed with lots of pillows, her TV on quietly in the corner.

'Are you OK?' I asked. 'Do you want me to wake up Mum?'

'No, thanks for coming home. I just don't feel very well and wanted you here,' she said, in between violent coughing spasms.

I climbed into bed next to her and we cuddled up the way we did when we were little girls. Within moments we'd both fallen asleep.

The next morning I took one look at Nicole and decided I was taking her to hospital. Wheezing and breathless, she was ghostly pale and had dark bags under her eyes. And each hacking cough seemed like it would rip her fragile body in two.

Dad was away working for a couple of weeks, and Mum had taken a job as a cleaner at a local police station, working the 6 to 9 a.m. shift so she could get back in time to get Nicole up and sort out her breakfast and medicines.

I texted her: *Nicole not well. Taking her to hospital. See you there when you finish work.* I typed hurriedly, keen to get Nicole to the hospital as soon as possible.

Nicole was so weak I had to help her get washed and dressed, packing a small overnight bag for her as I was sure she would be admitted for treatment.

At the hospital she was sent straight to the respiratory ward, where I helped settle her into a bed, after she'd been for a chest X-ray and had some blood tests done.

'You should go home,' she said later that afternoon to me and Mum, who'd rushed to the hospital straight from work. 'I'm really tired. I just want to go to sleep.'

Mum and I looked at one another. Normally, Nicole never wanted to be left alone in hospital; she was happiest when someone was there with her to chat to, or watch TV with. I couldn't remember a time when she'd ever asked to be left alone, and it unsettled me.

'Are you sure?' I asked. 'I don't mind staying.'

'No, go home. I'll be fine. I'm just shattered. I'll see you tomorrow,' she replied, her eyes already starting to close.

I went straight to Martin's, where I burst into tears as soon as I saw him. 'Something doesn't feel right,' I cried. 'I have a bad feeling.'

'But she's been in hospital lots of times and you've not been like this,' Martin said, cuddling me close to him.

'I know, but I can't shake the feeling that this time it's different. I can't explain it,' I said.

That night I stayed at home, sleeping in Nicole's bed to feel close to her. I think I saw every hour on the clock, waking constantly from bad dreams that she was calling for me and I couldn't find her. Eventually, I must have dozed off into a fitful sleep.

At 7 a.m. the landline rang.

Dad, who had travelled home the night before on hearing that Nicole had been admitted to hospital, answered it.

Sitting up in bed I listened intently, hoping it was good news and she was feeling better.

'OK … OK … we'll be right up,' he said, his voice grave.

I went ice-cold at the sound and leapt out of bed. 'What's happened, Dad? Is she OK?' I asked.

'She's not doing well. We need to go up to the hospital now,' he replied. 'They said they'd explain more when we got there.'

Dressing as fast as we could, Mum, Dad and I jumped into the car and drove quickly to Gartnavel. Gary was at work and we couldn't reach him, but I'm not sure he could have coped with being there.

The car was silent, each of us lost in our own worry about what we were going to find at the hospital. I cursed myself for having agreed to go home the day before and leave her alone. I should have stayed with her overnight. She shouldn't have been alone.

My heart sank when I saw Nicole's doctor and the ward sister waiting for us at the entrance to the ward. As they ushered us into the small relatives room my legs shook with fear. What were they going to tell us?

'Nicole has had a very bad night,' the doctor said, a worried look on his face. 'She has pneumonia, her blood-sugar levels are very unstable and she's in a very deep sleep right now – similar to a coma.'

'Is she going to be OK?' Mum asked, wiping away the tears that were streaming down her face.

'We really don't know. We're doing everything we can, but her condition is very serious,' the doctor replied.

'Can we take her home?' Dad asked.

'She wouldn't survive the journey, Mr Tennant. That's how unwell she is. We're doing our very best but we just don't know if she will pull through this time,' the doctor said quietly. 'I'm so sorry it's not better news.'

I felt dizzy, as if the room was spinning, and there was a roaring noise in my ears. I could hear Mum weeping uncontrollably, being comforted by the Sister, and the door slam as Dad walked out of the room. I knew he didn't want to break down in front of us.

All I could think about was Nicole: *we just don't know if she will pull through … we just don't know if she will pull through …* The doctor's words went around and around in my mind, but I was too shocked to cry. I felt completely numb, unable to take in what was happening.

There had been times over the years when I'd allowed myself, for a fleeting dark moment, to imagine what it would be like to lose Nicole, but I had always pushed those thoughts away, desperate to think that I would never find myself in that situation. Now it felt so surreal, in the most horrible way, to realise it might be happening.

Standing up shakily, in a daze, I followed the doctor to another private room, where Nicole was lying in bed, pale and lifeless, tubes snaking out of her arms and mouth.

The sight of her, my beautiful sister, woke me with a jolt from the shocked state I'd been in. I took her hand in mine. 'I'm here, 'Cole, can you hear me? They're wrong – you're not going anywhere, do you hear me? I'm not losing you, no way,' I whispered fiercely in her ear. I laid my head on her chest, hearing her laboured, wheezy breathing and began to cry, my tears soaking her pink pyjamas.

Mum stood opposite me stroking Nicole's hair gently, while Dad tickled her feet. 'Come on, sweetheart,' he said, his voice breaking. 'Wake up for us, we want to take you home.'

For the next couple of hours we sat around her bedside, talking to her and hoping she could hear us. Mum and Dad eventually left to collect Gary from his work, and to tell close family what was happening.

I stayed with Nicole. The room was quiet apart from the beeps of the machines to which she was hooked up. I didn't know what most of them did but it terrified me that she needed so many to help her. How could she have become so sick in 24 hours? I still couldn't take it in.

'Stay with me, Nicole … this can't be it.' I said, stroking her hand. 'I need you. We're a pair. Who am I without my sis?'

Mum and Dad returned, but without Gary.

'He wouldn't come,' Mum said, shaking her head. 'He said he couldn't face seeing her like this.'

At first, part of me was furious with him, but part of me also completely understood why he'd stayed away. He'd always run away from Nicole's problems, unable to deal with them, when the rest of us just had to, no matter how painful it was. But he did this because he loved her so, *so* much. He couldn't bear to watch his big sister get weaker and sicker by the day; it tore him apart inside.

While Nicole's and my bond was plain for all to see, Gary in his own quiet way had a very deep connection with her too. It was he who often stayed in to keep her company when I was at work or seeing friends, making her favourite meals or carrying her to her room if she was feeling too weak or tired to walk. From the little brother who had tortured her with pranks, he'd become a man who doted on her in a very unobtrusive way, as the dynamic of their relationship had changed to one where she needed him, instead of the other way around.

Knowing all this, I had to let go of my anger and understand it was too hard for Gary to come to the hospital. He wasn't being selfish, he just loved Nicole too much.

'Did I miss something? Is this my fault?' Mum kept asking, over and over. 'She was OK yesterday. I don't understand how this has all happened so fast …'

Leaving the room, I phoned our cousin Katrina from the corridor. 'I'm so frightened we're going to lose her,' I said. 'I've never seen her like this before.'

'She's a fighter, Melissa, she always has been. She'll get through this, I'm sure of it,' Katrina replied, refusing to accept this could be the end. 'I'm on my way to the hospital now.'

By the end of the day, Nicole's small hospital room was filled with Mum, Dad, me, Katrina, Nicole's friend, Alice, and other family members.

A few times Nicole half opened her eyes, but it was only fleeting before she'd slip into unconsciousness again. Watching her, I remembered how much we loved *Sleeping Beauty* as our bedtime story when we were little girls. Now all I wanted was for our princess to wake up. But I couldn't wave a magic spell over her – she had to fight this battle alone.

It grew dark outside and a nurse came to tell us only one person could stay with Nicole overnight.

'I'm staying,' Mum said firmly. 'Stewart, you and Melissa go home and come back in the morning.'

More than anything I wanted to stay but I knew Mum was determined not to leave Nicole, and there was no point in arguing with her. I kissed Nicole's forehead gently. 'Bye, sis, I'll see you in the morning,' I whispered in her ear.

Walking down the long hospital corridor I felt sick with fear I might have just said goodbye to my sister for the last time.

I prayed silently and fiercely that she would be there when I came back in the morning.

After a sleepless night, we all spent another day at Nicole's bedside, talking to her and playing her favourite music and TV programmes to try and bring her round.

That night I insisted I was staying with her. 'You go home and rest, Mum. I want to be here with her,' I said, when Mum tried to argue with me.

I didn't sleep a wink that night, just sat in a chair by her bedside watching her chest rise and fall. Her breathing was so laboured and erratic, it felt like each breath was a huge effort for her damaged lungs.

It was the longest night of my life as I willed her to fight for her life the way she had been doing since the moment we were born.

And then, as dawn broke over Glasgow, Nicole opened her eyes and turned to look at me, bleary and confused. Suddenly, she sat bolt upright in bed, pulling at one of the IV drips in her arm.

'Nurse! Nurse!' I shouted, leaping out of my chair. 'Can someone come? Quick!' Then I turned to Nicole. 'It's OK, Nicole, I'm here. You're in hospital, don't be frightened,' I said, as she looked around in confusion.

'What happened? Where am I?' she asked groggily.

I threw my arms around her. 'You're awake! Oh, Nicole … I was so scared!' I cried, hugging her tightly.

Suddenly the room filled with doctors and nurses, all checking her and exclaiming how much better she was doing.

'I don't remember anything,' Nicole said to me after we'd been left alone again, and I'd phoned Mum and Dad to tell them the good news. 'Was I really sick?'

I realised that telling her the truth would do no good, that it would only frighten her. She didn't need to know how close she had come to leaving us.

'No, no – you just needed some fluids and antibiotics,' I fibbed. 'You must have been really tired to have slept so deeply, but it's nothing to panic about.'

Nicole narrowed her eyes and I knew she knew I was playing down what had happened. 'You've never been a good liar, Melissa,' she said. Then she continued: 'I'm so sorry I scared everyone.' She paused. 'It's hard to explain, but I feel different. I'm tired of living under this cloud of getting sicker and sicker – something has to change. I want a life … a proper life. And I'm going to try my hardest to get one.'

Chapter Eight

Nicole spent a month in hospital recovering from pneumonia, and I visited her every single day.

Gradually, despite our best efforts to protect her from how seriously ill she'd been, she pieced together how close she had come to dying. It terrified her but also had a completely unexpected effect on her: it was as if one Nicole had gone into hospital and fallen into that coma-like sleep, and a completely different girl had awoken. Gone was her complacency about doing her breathing exercises and taking her medicines, gone were the flashes of jealousy and resentment, the bad moods and the anger that sometimes got her down. The animosity we'd all experienced – me more than anyone else – vanished.

It was as if she'd realised there was no point wasting her energy feeling bitter about the hand she'd been dealt, as it wasn't going to change anything. She'd come close to dying, and there was a steely determination in her eyes that she wasn't going to let it happen again.

'I've been sick all my life. Sickness is my "normal",' she told me one night, as we sat playing cards in her hospital room. 'I think I've been like this so long I've forgotten I *can* change this. It doesn't have to be this way forever. I just need to face it head-on and fight it.'

The following day she met with her doctor, insisting that me, Mum and Dad were there too.

'I want a transplant. I don't want to wait any longer – I'm just existing now, not living. I know it's the only chance I have of having a proper life,' she said. 'What do I need to do to get one? I'll do whatever you say.'

In the past, when she'd talked about transplants, her doctors had told her she was still too well for one. So when the doctor nodded in agreement, I was stunned.

'Yes, I think it's time we start thinking seriously about referring you for a transplant assessment,' he said.

Nicole was beaming, but I felt confused. Part of me was pleased: this was what she wanted, and she was right, it was her only chance of a normal life; but I also knew that this meant the disease was affecting her more than it ever had done before.

They wouldn't be considering her for a transplant unless she was seriously sick.

'If you're serious about wanting a transplant, you need to work with us to get you on that list,' the doctor went on. 'You need to gain some weight, do your physiotherapy and breathing exercises, and keep your diabetes well controlled. OK?' he said.

'I promise,' she replied. 'Whatever it takes, I'll do it.'

I reached over and squeezed her hand. 'We'll all be behind you, Nicole. Every step of the way.'

A month after Nicole had been admitted to hospital, she was allowed to go home, but joining her was an oxygen tank and a wheelchair.

The first time I saw her in the chair, being pushed down the hospital corridor by Dad, it felt like the wind had been knocked out of me. How had we got to this point? It felt like so long ago that Mum and Dad were reassuring me cystic fibrosis just meant she had a bad cough. Now it was actually disabling her.

At home she didn't need the chair, but she couldn't walk to the end of the street any more; she had become so breathless and weak that she had to be pushed in the wheelchair whenever she left the house. And the oxygen tank went everywhere with her, as she needed it more and more.

I *hated* the sight of the tank and the chair.

They were tangible evidence of how sick Nicole was, sicker than she'd been before, and how aggressively her cystic fibrosis was starting to affect her. And when we went out, people stared at her, which drove me crazy, the look in their eyes one of pity.

'Calm down, Melissa,' Nicole told me as I pushed her home from the local shops, fuming after overhearing an elderly woman whisper, 'What a shame' to her friend, when she'd seen Nicole.

'It just really bugs me,' I seethed. 'Haven't they ever seen someone in a wheelchair before?'

'Yes, but probably not anyone as gorgeous as me, eh?' Nicole chuckled, once again finding something to laugh about when she had every right to feel down.

I knew how determined she was to get a transplant, and her utter faith that if she fulfilled her part of the deal by looking after herself, she would get a new set of lungs. But, once again, that dark feeling of uncertainty and dread haunted me, keeping me awake at night.

Her cystic fibrosis was a ticking time bomb. None of us knew how long she could continue to live with it, and whether she'd get a transplant in time. And I knew that even if she did everything the doctors said, and was put on the transplant list, that was only the beginning. I'd been secretly researching lung transplants and learned there's a serious shortage of donor lungs in the UK: only a couple of hundred people get a transplant every year. The odds were massively stacked against my sister.

Nicole knew the odds too, but she was adamant she was going to be one of the success stories.

I hated myself for being so filled with doubt, as if I was somehow jinxing it, especially when everyone else was so positive about a transplant too. And so I kept my research secret, and in front of her I couldn't have been more enthusiastic about it.

What amazed me was how Nicole managed to hang on to her optimism and positivity, at a time when her day-to-day life had never been so restricted by her illness.

'You're terrible at this!' she jokingly scolded me, as I pushed her in her wheelchair to a local coffee shop one Saturday morning. 'You need to work on your steering!' She giggled. 'Hey, I know, why don't we dress up as Lou and Andy from *Little Britain* for Halloween this year?'

I had no idea how she could laugh and joke when she should have been completely frustrated at being so dependent on others, even just to leave the house.

Every day I felt in awe of her spirit.

Even part-time work was out of the question now for Nicole – she was stuck at home most of the week, apart from when one of us would take her shopping or out for a meal, if she felt well enough.

I was still splitting my time between home and Martin's house, but I tried to see her every day and, as always, our family rallied round, always popping in to spend time with her. But, apart from me and Martin, and Craig, who she was still really close to, and her friend Alice, gradually Nicole became even more isolated from her friends.

'I understand,' she said softly, when I asked her if she was cross that friends had stopped calling to the house to see her. 'People are busy with their own lives. They're not able to come and sit with me all the time.'

But I hated seeing her so cut off from the world around her. Nicole now practically lived in her bedroom, watching TV and playing with her dogs on her bed. Now, just like when she was younger, Mum's days once again revolved around caring for her.

Not long after she was discharged from hospital, Nicole began to suffer from blinding headaches. Doctors couldn't explain what was causing them, and it was a vicious circle as the more oxygen she needed, the worse the headaches became. Hunched over like an old lady, there were days she lay in bed in agony when even the morphine she was prescribed barely touched the pain.

Nicole was also being prescribed large doses of steroids. One of their side effects was to make her look bloated, and cause her hair to fall out. My sister had always taken a lot of care with her appearance but the sicker she became, the harder she found it to maintain her look, and it was one of the few things to really get her down. Most days she wasn't well enough to bath or shower herself and needed Mum or me to help her get washed and dressed. Just putting on some make-up and brushing her hair was an effort, and she lived in pyjamas because she went out so little.

One day, in the summer of 2012, I took her out to the local park in her wheelchair to get some fresh air. The sun was shining and it felt good to see Nicole outside, a rare flush of pink in her cheeks.

'I want to go home, Melissa,' she said suddenly, as I pushed her through the park towards an ice-cream van that had parked at the entrance.

'What are you talking about?' I asked. 'We just got here. What's wrong?'

I followed Nicole's gaze to a group of little boys who'd been playing football near us.

'Why's her face so fat?' one asked me, pointing at Nicole.

'And what's that tube going up her nose?' said another.

This was the last thing Nicole needed, her self-confidence about how she looked already low.

'They're just wee boys, Nicole. They don't mean any harm. Ignore them. Come on, let's go and get an ice-cream.'

'No, Melissa, take me home. I mean it,' Nicole snapped. 'I look terrible. No wonder they're staring at me.'

Pushing her home, I was devastated. Hunched over in her chair, I knew Nicole was trying hard not to cry, embarrassed about what had happened. I didn't know what to say to make her feel better. I knew she wouldn't believe me if I'd said she was always beautiful to me.

On days like this I felt like screaming with frustration. My sense of helplessness was unbearable and, seeing her in pain, or depressed about how she looked, ripped right through me.

Despite the few occasions in our childhood, I'd never really bought into that belief that twins can feel one another's pain, but increasingly I started to think there might be some truth in it. Because when Nicole had a 'bad day', so did I. While hers was a physical pain, mine was an emotional one.

Wanting to spend as much time as I could with her, I stopped going out at weekends so I could stay in with Nicole and keep her company.

'How come you're not going out tonight?' she asked me one Saturday night.

'I can't be bothered. I'm too tired from work,' I lied. 'I'll just hang out with you instead.'

'I'll loan you money if you're skint,' she offered. 'Or do you want to borrow an outfit from me? You've worked hard all week, you should go out and enjoy yourself.'

'No, honestly. I'm happy just staying in,' I said, amazed at how different she was from the Nicole who'd been so resentful of my social life not all that long ago.

Nicole was continuing to be a model patient: eating well, allowing Mum to do her physio again and taking all her medicines. Slowly her weight increased to 41kg, the target her doctors had given her, and although she still looked very fragile, they were pleased with her progress, and promised she'd be referred for a transplant assessment soon.

It was all she thought and talked about. Every other sentence out of her mouth began with, 'When I get my transplant …' Her life post-transplant became her focus, her only goal – when she talked about the things she wanted to do, her face lit up with anticipation.

But I knew there was no guarantee she'd get to live this life she dreamed of. Looking at her, so fragile, and with a constant cough, dependent on an oxygen tank and a wheel-chair, it was hard to imagine her ever being well enough to fulfil all these dreams she had. And I hated myself for even thinking like that. Was I being pessimistic or realistic? I didn't know any more.

I craved Nicole's confidence and pushed my negative thoughts to the back of my mind.

In October 2012, Nicole and I turned 21.

It had been such a difficult year for her I was determined this birthday was going to be all about Nicole, and whatever she wanted I would make it happen.

Fancy-dress crazy as always, she decided on a masquerade theme for the party, to be held at a local bowling club. Together we went shopping and I picked out a black and gold halter-neck dress, while she went for a black and white dress with a peplum skirt, both accessorised with dramatic masks.

Now permanently dependent on her oxygen tank, Nicole had no choice but to wear it over her costume, strapped to her back.

'I'm going to look really silly, aren't I?' she grumbled, as we got ready for the party.

I stood in front of the mirror, carefully applying my mascara and lipstick. 'Hmm, maybe we should have had a different theme and you could have gone as a Ghostbuster,' I teased her, determined nothing was going to get in the way of her enjoying this night.

'You cheeky cow!' she laughed, her face lighting up.

My heart soared on hearing her giggle, it was so rarely heard any more.

At the party, all our family and friends mingled, wearing amazing, ornate masks. I'd arranged for the DJ to play all of Nicole's favourite cheesy pop music all night but, breathless and weak, she barely took to the dancefloor. Instead, she sat in her wheelchair while a steady stream of people came to talk to her.

Watching her, I couldn't help but think back to our eighteenth birthday party, just three years before. It felt like only yesterday, but so much had changed. And the contrast in my sister then and now was heartbreaking. Unless you'd known then about her illness, you might not have guessed she was ill. She'd danced, got a bit tipsy and had been the life and soul of the party. Fast-forward three years and she'd been ravaged by her illness. Anyone could see how unwell she was as she sat hunched and swollen in her wheelchair, coughing every few minutes into a hanky.

Despite how unwell she looked, though, there was a twinkle in her eye that night. She knew she had defied the doctors' expectations, who'd told Mum when she was diagnosed as a baby that she might not live past the age of 20. And she had cheated death earlier that year, recovering from pneumonia when we'd been told she might not make it.

I was sure Nicole was convinced that this would be her last birthday party before her lung transplant, and that this time next year she'd be up there on the dancefloor with everyone else celebrating.

I hoped so much that she was right.

Chapter Nine

In May 2013, exactly a year after Nicole had almost died from pneumonia, came the news she had been so desperate for.

Checking my mobile phone during my lunch break at work, I listened to a voicemail from my sister: 'Melissa, call me back! I'm being sent for a transplant assessment and I want you to come with me!'

I dialled her number immediately, my hands shaking with adrenaline. For such a long time I had felt so doubtful we'd ever reach this point … now it was happening, I could hardly believe it.

'I got a letter in the post this morning, telling me I have to go to a hospital in Newcastle this month, for three days. They'll do lots of tests on me and then hopefully will put my name on the transplant list,' she said excitedly. 'Only one person can come with me and I want it to be you, Melissa.'

'What about Mum?' I replied. 'She'll definitely want to go with you.'

'I don't think she'll handle it as well as you. I think she might get emotional, and you'll be calmer. That's what I'm going to need.'

I was really touched Nicole wanted me to be there with her, but I knew Mum would insist on going.

'It'll look like I'm a terrible mother if I'm not there with you, Nicole,' Mum said over dinner that night. 'I need to be there with you. I *want* to be there with you.'

I could tell Nicole felt torn between wanting me there and not wanting to hurt Mum's feelings, and the last thing I wanted was for her and Mum to fall out at a time when we all needed to pull together.

'It's really sweet of you to want me there, Nicole, but I don't think I could get the time off work at such short notice,' I lied. 'Maybe it's best if Mum goes instead—?'

Mum looked at me gratefully. 'Thank you,' she silently mouthed, when Nicole wasn't looking.

As much as I would have given anything to go with Nicole, and support her, I knew that after 21 years of fighting cystic fibrosis alongside Nicole, Mum needed to be there. Like Nicole, she was so confident about a transplant, and so sure these tests were the final hurdle to get over before a set of new lungs could be found, she wanted to be with her when she scaled that hurdle.

At first, Nicole was so excited about her trip to Newcastle, packing and repacking her case – it was as if she was going away on holiday as she giddily chattered about what the hospital would be like. She couldn't wait to meet these new doctors who she was sure would give her the green light for a transplant. She'd been told that the assessment would involve everything from checking her BMI and blood tests, to multiple X-rays and scans, and exercise tests to establish her lung-function.

'I can't believe it's actually happening,' she said, as I helped her pick out some of her favourite pairs of Disney-themed pyjamas for her hospital stay. 'Normally I dread being admitted to hospital, but this time I can't wait. It feels like the beginning of something exciting, doesn't it? Finally, things are going to change for me, I'm sure of it.'

And we had all been sworn to secrecy by Nicole, forbidden from telling anyone she was going to be assessed. 'I want it to be a surprise when I come back and can tell people I'm on the list,' she explained. 'We should have a party to celebrate when I get back!'

But the night before she left, for the first time ever, doubt started to creep into her mind. 'What if the doctors say I can't go on the list?' she asked me anxiously. 'What then?'

'Well, that could just mean you're not ill enough for a transplant and that would be a good thing, in a way,' I said, trying to put a positive spin on it to stop her worrying.

'Hmm … I suppose. But I really, *really* hope they put me on the list, don't you? I can't even contemplate them saying no.'

'Of course I do. And I'm sure they will put you on it,' I reassured her. 'Give me a hug, I'm going to miss you. I think this is the longest we've ever been apart, you know.'

The following day an ambulance collected Mum and Nicole from Gartnavel for the two-and-a-half-hour journey to Newcastle.

I waved them off, biting my lip to stop the tears that were welling up inside me. For a moment I wished I'd gone along with Nicole's wish for me to go with her. I'd always been there, every time she'd been admitted to hospital, and it felt strange knowing I wouldn't be there with her this time. But I felt so emotional, I wasn't sure I'd have been much of a support to her. I'd never felt so nervous in all my life, and I couldn't begin to imagine how Nicole was feeling as she sped down the motorway, knowing that the next three days would hopefully completely change her life.

The next day I checked my phone at work every five minutes, eager to hear how Nicole's assessment was going.

At four o'clock, Mum called.

'How's it going?' I asked. 'Is she getting on OK?'

'They can't do the tests. She's got a chest infection and isn't well enough,' she said despondently. I could tell she was trying not to cry.

I couldn't speak, I was so shocked.

'Can't they wait until she's better and test her then?' I asked finally, hopeful there was still a chance it hadn't been a wasted trip.

Mum was silent.

'What's wrong?' I asked, growing worried.

'It's not that simple …' she said after a long silence. Mum went on to explain that after examining Nicole, the doctors had sat them both down. 'I knew from their faces it was bad news,' she said. 'They said she wasn't well enough for all the tests. So I asked if we could come back when she was. But they explained she's just too sick for a transplant – she wouldn't survive the operation. It's not going to happen. They've even suggested she be put on a ventilator to help her breathe, but apart from that there's nothing more that can be done for her …' Mum said quietly, breaking down.

It was the worst-case scenario.

Nicole had crossed that very fine and cruel line between being sick enough to be considered for a transplant, and too sick to survive the operation. Her chance was gone, her dream of a transplant shattered. There was no more hope, nowhere to turn to now.

'How's Nicole?' I asked, when I finally found my voice again.

'At first she was really defiant. After the meeting she turned to me and said, "I'm not going to die, Mum. I'm not. I'm going to get better and come back down here." But I think it's starting to kick in now. She's just lying in her bed, not talking. She's crushed.'

All my dark thoughts I'd hidden for years – that Nicole would never get a transplant – rushed to the front of my mind. They had come true. I felt physically sick.

Was this my fault? Had I somehow jinxed her chances by feeling so doubtful and anxious for so long, when she had been so confident and positive?

I knew I was being stupid: this was nothing to do with me and my secret fears I'd kept from her, but I still felt wracked with guilt. All I wanted was Nicole home now, not hundreds of miles away, dealing with such devastating news without me.

Hanging up the phone, I sank into a chair in the staffroom.

It was now just a matter of when, not if, I lost my beautiful sister to this horrific disease.

The next day Nicole arrived home by ambulance, with Mum. As soon as I saw her I knew something had changed deep within her. Where there had been hope and anticipation when she had left two days before, now there was nothing but defeat.

The light had gone out in her eyes.

As she shuffled slowly the few yards from the ambulance into the house, she stared down at the ground, her tear-stained face completely expressionless. She was like a zombie, and I could practically feel the intense sadness radiating from her.

I lay down on her bed beside her. We didn't speak – I think both of us realised there was nothing to say. I slept that night beside her, needing to be as close to her as I could.

Nicole had been sick when she left for Newcastle, but when she came back she seemed so much worse. She had no fight left in her; she'd given up the hope that had been keeping her going for the past year. It was as if losing that emotional battle had sucked away her very last physical strength: her hair was thinner than ever and kept falling out in clumps, she hunched over in pain, her bloated face often contorted in agony when violent coughs ripped through her.

A few days after she came back from Newcastle I knocked gently on her bedroom door. 'Nicole, do you fancy a cuppa? I've just put the kettle on,' I said.

There was no reply but, listening at the door, I heard muffled sobs.

Opening the door, I saw Nicole kneeling on the floor of her bedroom, shaking violently and crying.

'What's wrong, Nicole? What's happened?' I asked, kneeling beside her.

She looked at me, her blue eyes that had once been so full of mischief and fun now dulled with pain.

'I can't do this any more, Melissa. I can't live like this,' she said, breaking down again in my arms. 'It's a living hell. I have nothing – not my health, not a future … nothing. What did I do to deserve this?'

I stroked her hair, desperately trying to find some words that would comfort her or shake her out of this black hole of despair she'd been sucked into. But what could I say? I knew she was right: now that her only chance at a proper future had been robbed from her, I understood why she was so distraught.

And, more than anything, I felt guilty that I had been born the healthy twin. Nature had picked her to be the one with cystic fibrosis when it could so easily have been me. In that moment, as we knelt together on the floor of her room, I would have done anything to swap places with her, to give her my healthy lungs, my life and my future.

'Come on, sis, don't cry. You've always been so strong! You need to just find that strength inside you again. I know you can do it,' I said.

But the truth was I didn't know how much strength she had left.

After her return from Newcastle, Nicole's conversations about what she was going to do in the future stopped completely. There was no more scribbling of ideas in her diary or daydreaming about the countries she would visit and the challenges she'd take on. She spent most of her time in bed, too weak or too unhappy to even get up.

Working full-time, I dashed home after every shift so I could spend every spare moment with her. She had good days, and bad days, when the smallest thing could make her cry.

One evening, after I'd helped her have a bubble bath, I sat brushing her hair gently.

'I'm never going to get the chance to just brush my hair normally, and not have to watch clumps of it fall out, am I?' she asked sadly.

I couldn't look her in the eye. We both knew time was running out, that her body was giving up. That her dreams of a normal life were never going to become a reality.

I tried so hard to keep upbeat as I knew she didn't need to see me falling apart, and it felt selfish to indulge my own fears when she was coping with so much. Mum and Dad were the same but they were struggling too, watching their wee girl slip away before their eyes.

Later that evening I stood in the kitchen with Mum, helping her make dinner.

'You're very quiet. Are you OK?' she asked.

'I just helped Nicole take a bath, and huge clumps of her hair came out as I brushed it, Mum,' I said. 'She's falling apart in front of us.'

Mum suddenly gripped the worktop tightly.

'Mum, what's wrong? I asked, alarmed.

She looked up at me, her eyes welling with sudden tears. 'I can't do this … I can't do this,' she sobbed. 'I can't watch my baby girl suffer like this. How much more is she supposed to endure?'

I hugged Mum tightly, stroking her hair the way she used to mine when I was a little girl. 'Come on, Mum. We all need to hold it together. For Nicole's sake,' I whispered.

First Nicole, now Mum. My family was falling apart under the strain of this terrible disease. I didn't know how much longer we could hold on. I felt utterly helpless, and sick with dread about how much worse it could possibly get for us all.

Chapter Ten

Months before Nicole was rejected for a lung transplant, Martin and I had booked a week-long holiday to Fuengirola in Spain, renting a villa with his parents, Rita and Gerry, and other relatives of his.

It was to be our first holiday together and also my first without Nicole, as before then I'd only been abroad on family breaks.

It was Nicole who'd encouraged me to go: 'You work so hard, and you've been spending so much of your time looking after me, you need a break, Melissa,' she'd said, when I'd been deliberating over whether or not I should book a flight.

It wasn't that I didn't want to spend time with Martin, and the thought of that and lying by a pool in the sun sounded amazing, but even a week felt like a long time to be away from my sister. Eventually, though, she persuaded me that I needed the break, and once I'd booked the flights I was really excited about working on my tan, going for cocktails and having some quality time with Martin.

But when Nicole came home from Newcastle, so unwell and so crushed by the news that she wasn't going to be placed on the transplant list, I immediately began to have serious doubts about leaving her.

'How can I fly off to Spain to enjoy myself when she's like this?' I said to Martin, the week before we were due to go. 'She needs me here with her. What if she gets even sicker and I'm thousands of miles away?'

'You need some time off, Melissa,' Martin said. 'You're exhausted with worry, you're not sleeping. You need to relax for a few days, or you're not going to be any use to Nicole.'

He was right. I was shattered with the effort of working full-time, helping Mum care for Nicole and worrying about her constantly. But I felt guilty about jetting off to the sun when my sister was stuck at home, now almost permanently attached to her oxygen tank, rarely able to leave the house.

When I confessed to Nicole that I was thinking about cancelling my holiday, she was cross.

'No way, Melissa! I'm not having this. You've paid for your holiday, you've been working really hard and you're always here for me. It's time you had some time for yourself and Martin,' she said firmly, her pale, thin arms folded in a way that let me know she meant business. 'I've held you back too many times, and I'm not going to be the reason you miss your holiday. You're going, and that's that. I don't want to hear anything more about it. OK?'

I nodded reluctantly. When Nicole had made her mind up about something there was no point in arguing with her. But no matter how hard I tried to get excited about the holiday and reassure myself that Nicole would be fine without me, I couldn't shake off the feeling that I shouldn't go.

I took Nicole out for lunch the day before I went to Spain, to her favourite restaurant, Tony Roma's, but even that failed to lift her spirits.

As she pushed her ribs around her plate, I chatted about the clothes I'd bought for my holiday and how Mum had given me a lecture on using a high-factor sun cream because of my porcelain pale skin, which was just like Nicole's. I could hear myself rabbiting on, trying to fill the silences because Nicole was so quiet.

'Are you OK?' I asked eventually.

'I'm just really tired. Would you mind if we went home now?' she replied, her meal barely touched.

I didn't dare raise the possibility of me not going away again, knowing it would only upset her, but seeing her so low just made the thought of leaving her the next day even harder.

The following morning, on a Friday in early July 2013, I zipped up my case and waited for Martin to collect me to go to the airport for our flight.

Nicole was in bed so I went into her room to say goodbye. 'I'm going now,' I said. 'Are you sure you don't want me to stay?'

'Don't be crazy. Go and enjoy yourself, get an amazing tan and don't forget to bring me back lots of pressies, OK?'

'OK, I promise, Miss Bossy Boots,' I said with a laugh. Sitting on the edge of her bed, I hugged Nicole tight. She was so thin and fragile she felt like a doll in my arms, and I could hear her wheezing with every breath she took. 'See you in a week, Nicole,' I said.

'Have a brilliant holiday,' she replied. 'Don't worry about me – I'll be here when you get back.'

Outside I heard Martin beep the horn of his car.

Closing Nicole's bedroom door behind me, I felt sick to the pit of my stomach. Every part of me wanted to turn around, unpack my case and stay with her, but I knew she'd be furious, and Martin would be gutted. 'Come on, Melissa,' I said to myself. 'Stop being silly. It's only a week, then you'll be home.'

Waiting in the airport bar for our flight that afternoon everyone was in high spirits, excited at the thought of the week ahead. Determined not to be a downer on everyone's fun, I plastered a fake smile on my face and sipped my glass of champagne.

'Here's to a great holiday,' Martin said, clinking everyone's glasses.

I made a silent wish: 'Here's to Nicole, and getting home to her as soon as I can.'

It should have been an amazing holiday. The villa was luxurious, with its own private pool, and Martin and I had a gorgeous bedroom with a little balcony outside to sit on. Each day, everyone snoozed by the pool, read and took little walks to the bars and restaurants nearby for coffee and long lunches, but I just couldn't relax. I was on edge all the time, thinking constantly about Nicole, and spent a lot of time alone in the bedroom because I didn't want to spoil the fun for everyone else by being in such a low mood.

It was on the Wednesday after I'd flown out to Spain that we spoke on FaceTime. I wasn't able to get any texts on my mobile but the villa had wi-fi, which meant Nicole and I could FaceTime one another using our iPhones.

At first Nicole seemed OK, asking me how the holiday was going and what I'd been up to. But when I asked her how she was feeling, she suddenly burst into tears. 'I'm not feeling very well, La La. I'm hardly off my oxygen now, and I'm so tired all the time,' she wept.

'I'm going to be home really soon,' I said, desperately trying not to cry. 'And once I'm back, you and I are just going to cuddle up together on the sofa, with LouLou and Ralph, until you're feeling better. Just hang in there until I get back, OK?'

'I will.' She nodded. 'I can't wait to see you, Sis.'

'Me too,' I replied. 'I miss you, Nicole.' I hung up, wracked with helplessness.

I didn't know that would be the last conversation I'd ever have with my sister.

I didn't sleep well that night, imagining Nicole at home without me, feeling so ill. Tossing and turning for hours, I felt so guilty that I hadn't heeded my instinct and stayed with her.

The next day I sat in the shade, trying to read a book but too tired and anxious to really concentrate. Going into the villa to get a drink, I noticed I had a private Facebook message from Katrina.

Hi, Melissa. Can you please phone me? was all it said.

In my dread, I dropped my phone, and it clattered off the tiled floor. Running back outside, I threw myself into Martin's arms. 'She's gone … she's gone …' I screamed over and over. 'Nicole's gone …'

'Oh, my God,' Martin gasped, rocking me in his arms. 'Are you sure? What's happened?'

I explained about the Facebook message. 'Katrina wouldn't have contacted me unless something terrible had happened,' I said.

'You don't know what's happened, it might be nothing. Let's call Katrina and find out what's going on,' Martin said.

My legs were shaking so hard I could hardly walk, and he half-carried me back into the villa, everyone else following behind, completely silent.

My hands trembling, I picked up my phone from the floor and dialled Katrina's number. 'Is she gone?' I asked, as soon as she answered.

'Melissa, you need to come home as soon as you can,' Katrina said.

'Tell me now, has she gone?' I asked again, desperation in my voice.

'No ...' Katrina replied.

I dropped the phone again as the intense relief that my sister was alive hit me.

But my feeling was to be short-lived.

Martin's mum, Rita, picked up the phone and as she listened to Katrina speaking, I could see from her face that something was dreadfully wrong. Hanging up the phone, she turned to me.

'We need to get you home as quickly as possible,' she said.

'She's not going to make it, is she? Tell me the truth,' I cried.

'They're not sure ... she's very poorly ...' she replied, shaking her head, wringing her hands together. 'I'm so sorry, love. Katrina is booking you and Martin on a flight home tonight. There's no time to waste.'

I was paralysed with grief and sat on the sofa like a statue as Martin jumped up and started barking orders to everyone to pack my case and get our passports out of the safe.

As everyone ran around me, I sat thinking about Nicole. Was she in pain? Was she conscious? Did she know I was coming back to her? And one question went around and around in my mind: would I make it home in time to say goodbye to her?

Within an hour we were in a taxi, speeding down the motorway to Malaga Airport.

I held Martin's hand tightly as we both sat in silence, willing the car to go faster. He kept glancing over at me, and I knew he was waiting for me to break down, but the truth was I was too frightened now to cry. Frightened that my worst nightmare was coming true: I was going to lose my sister, and I wouldn't be with her at the end.

Making it to the airport with minutes to spare before check-in closed, we raced to the departure gate. We'd been in such a rush to leave the villa I was still wearing the shorts and T-shirt I'd been in all day, and as I tried to run through the departure gate my flip-flops kept coming off. At the gate I stopped, out of breath from pulling my case behind me, carrying my flip-flops in my hand.

I started to laugh.

'What's so funny?' said Martin, shocked to see me laughing.

'Nicole would be in stitches if she could see me now, looking like a mess and racing around like a headless chicken,' I said.

And I hoped so desperately I would get the chance to tell her all about our airport dash, to hear her laugh and see her smile again.

The plane journey was only three hours long but it felt like an eternity. Every minute was like an hour as I stared out the window.

'This isn't the way it's meant to be,' I said to Martin. 'I'm meant to be with her. I've always been with her, from the moment we were born.' I shook my head. 'I should never have left her.'

'We're going to make it,' he reassured me, but both of us knew there was no guarantee.

For all we knew she had already died.

I tried to read to pass the time but I couldn't concentrate on anything but the minutes ticking past on my watch. Instead, I spent the rest of the flight with my eyes closed, sending mental messages to Nicole.

If ever there was a time to believe in our twin bond it was now, and I willed her to know that I was nearly home, to hang on for me.

As soon as we landed I switched on my mobile phone, dreading a message from Katrina or Mum telling me I was too late.

Suddenly a message flashed up on my screen. It was from Nicole: *Hi, sis. I miss you. Can't wait to see you! Xxx* it read.

A huge smile broke out across my face. 'She must be OK!' I exclaimed. 'Look, she's just texted me.' Then I looked at the date of the text. It had been sent three days ago, but because I'd had no mobile phone reception in Spain I had only just received it. In a split second, my relief turned to devastation and that glimmer of hope I'd had for a moment that she was OK was crushed.

'Come on,' said Martin. 'Let's go. Paul's texted me. He's waiting at Arrivals to drive us to the hospital.'

When I saw my cousin I ran to him and we hugged. 'How is she?' I asked, dreading his answer.

He hesitated. 'She was fine yesterday ... no one knows how this happened so fast,' he stuttered.

'Is she still here?' I asked. 'That's all I need to know.'

He nodded. 'Yes. We think … we think she's waiting for you.'

'Let's go then. She needs me,' I said.

As Paul's car sped through the night-time streets of Glasgow, I wiped my tears away. Nicole needed me to be strong. It was time to face my very worst nightmare.

It was time to say goodbye.

Chapter Eleven

As Paul's car pulled into the hospital car park I opened the door before he'd even come to a stop.

Through the darkness, towards the brightly-lit hospital entrance I ran, willing my legs to move faster, conscious that every second counted.

I raced down the hospital corridors, squinting in the harsh strip lighting after the darkness outside. The antiseptic hospital smell, the muffled sounds of machines bleeping, nurses murmuring words of comfort to their patients was so familiar, but I had never before felt such fear in my heart, in all my years of going there. It felt like someone had reached into my chest, grabbed my heart and was twisting it. The terror of being too late, and not getting to Nicole in time, propelled me forward, faster and faster.

I knew Gartnavel Hospital like the back of my hand after six years of visiting Nicole there, and I headed straight to the private room near the respiratory ward, which Paul had told me she was in.

My heart was thumping as hard as it could go as I reached the door, partly from running but also from trepidation about what was waiting for me on the other side. Would my sister still be alive? Or would I have missed spending her last moments with her, and my chance to say goodbye? So frightened it would be the latter, I could hardly bring myself to open the door.

Taking a deep breath, I walked into the room.

There were so many people gathered around the bed I couldn't see Nicole at first: Mum, Dad, Gary, my cousins Dianne, Christine and John were all there, standing, or sitting on hard plastic chairs on each side of the hospital bed. Without speaking, they all stood back as I walked towards her.

Nicole lay sleeping on her right-hand side.

When I saw she was still alive my legs nearly gave way beneath me with relief. I wasn't too late, I'd made it.

Curled up in the foetal position, Nicole looked even smaller and more fragile than she had before I left for Spain, her skin deathly pale with dark shadows under her eyes. Apart from an oxygen mask over her face, there were no tubes, wires or machines attached to her, but as I neared the bed I could hear her breathing was laboured and raspy, her chest rising and falling erratically.

I felt confused. She looked so peaceful, dressed in her favourite pink Disney pyjamas, she could easily have been asleep in her own bed at home. Why were there no signs of her being treated? Where were the IVs of medicine? Why wasn't her heart-rate being monitored?

Weren't they trying to save her?

Looking around at everyone's tearful faces, I was shocked when a sudden and completely unexpected feeling of deep anger swept over me. They had all been here with her when it should have been *me*. So much time had been wasted travelling home from Spain – hours I could have spent with Nicole. Now, it was clear time was running out and I felt cheated.

I should have trusted my twin instinct and never left her.

Someone placed a chair by the bed for me, beside her head, and I sat down. 'I'm here, Nicole,' I whispered in her ear, taking her hand in mine, her skin cool to the touch. 'I love you.'

Suddenly her whole body jerked and her long eyelashes fluttered.

Everyone gasped.

'She can hear you,' Mum said. 'That's the first time she's moved all day!'

I began to cry, overwhelmed at the thought Nicole could somehow hear me and was trying to let me know. 'Wake up, Nicole, please,' I begged her. 'Just open your eyes for me.'

But she was perfectly still again, the only sound in the room her wheezing breaths.

I looked around at Mum and Dad. They stood, arms wrapped round one another, their faces pale and tear-stained. 'What happened?' I asked.

'Last night she was feeling very unwell and struggling to breathe, so we phoned for an ambulance and she was rushed here,' Mum explained. 'When we arrived, they sent Dad and me off for a coffee while they ran tests on her. I knew something was different this time, I just had an awful feeling.' Mum swallowed. 'When we got back to the ward, a doctor took us into a private room and that's when he told us …' She stopped, breaking down into wracking sobs.

Dad hugged her, kissing the top of her head gently as she wept on his shoulder. 'He told us that she wasn't going to make it,' Dad continued. 'Her body can't take in enough oxygen because her lungs are so damaged, so her organs are failing. She isn't going to get better.' He fell silent, staring at the floor. 'We just have to wait now. They can't do anything more for her …'

I looked at Nicole. Every breath she took seemed to be weaker and weaker, as if she was slipping away right in front of us.

'Why didn't anyone call me sooner?' I asked, angrily. 'Why did you wait? I could have had longer with her.'

No one spoke, or made eye contact with me, probably shocked at my outburst.

It was Katrina who spoke. 'We just didn't know what to do for the best, Melissa. Please understand – it all happened so fast. But then one of Nicole's doctors told us that when his father was dying, his brother didn't call him in time, and he'd never forgiven him for that. So we knew we had to bring you home.'

I turned back to Nicole, stroking her hair and watching her chest rise and fall so feebly. And then: 'I don't want to stay,' I suddenly blurted out, the words out of my mouth before I'd really thought about what I was saying.

'What do you mean?' Mum said, visibly shocked. 'Don't you want to be with her … at the end?'

'I don't want to remember her like this, I can't bear to see her go.' I stood up so suddenly, my chair toppled over, crashing to the floor. 'I thought I would want to be here but … but I just can't do it,' I said.

No one said a word. They just looked at me, completely stunned and bewildered.

I knew they couldn't believe that after my desperate dash back from Spain I wasn't going to stay. I could hardly believe what I was feeling myself but, deep down inside, I knew it was the right thing to do.

I knew if I watched Nicole die it would haunt me for ever. And I didn't want that awful moment when she took her last breath to be my last memory of my sister. Our lives started together, inside Mum, and we were born together on the same day, but I just couldn't share her death with her. I couldn't.

And I knew she would understand.

She had always been the brave one of the two of us, the one to lead and face things head-on. More than anyone, Nicole would understand I just couldn't cope seeing her die.

'Are you sure, Melissa?' Dad asked. 'Is this definitely what you want?'

I nodded slowly. 'I just can't … she'll understand, I know she will,' I whispered. I leaned over and kissed Nicole on the cheek. 'Bye, 'Cole … I love you,' I said. 'I'm sorry, please understand.'

Her eyelashes fluttered again and I desperately hoped it was a sign she could hear me, and was giving me her permission to leave.

Stumbling out of the room, Martin was waiting for me in the corridor, silent and grim-faced. I knew he was battling his own grief: he loved Nicole like a sister.

'I'll take you home,' he said, as I leant on him, physically weak with the weight of my grief.

Gary followed me out of the room and the three of us drove home in complete silence, too lost in our own pain to speak.

Martin and Gary sat in the living room while I washed my face, put on my pyjamas and lay on Nicole's bed, cuddling her teddies to me. Images of her in that hospital bed kept flashing through my mind, so instead I took out an old photo album and looked at pictures of us splashing about in the swimming pool on holiday in Tenerife when we were six, and dressed up as Pongo and Perdi from *101 Dalmations* the Halloween we were four. In every photo we had our arms wrapped round one another, smiling contentedly. We were so happy and innocent, with no idea that the disease Nicole carried inside her would lead us to this terrible night.

At 2.30 a.m. the phone rang shrilly in the silent house. I heard Martin answer it after just two rings.

Running into the hall from Nicole's bedroom, I took one look at his face and collapsed on the floor. 'She's gone, isn't she?' I screamed hysterically.

Hanging up the phone, all he could do was nod, wrapping his arms around me.

A searing pain tore through my body, as if the bond that had connected Nicole and me for 21 years was being ripped in two.

'She died a few moments ago,' Martin said. 'She just slipped away.'

Nicole had died with just Mum, Dad and our older cousin, John, with her.

It was Friday, 12 July, and I knew I would never, as long as I lived, forget this date.

As Martin held me, rocking me in his arms, my body shook violently as I went into a deep shock. It felt like I was falling into darkness as agonising grief pulsed through me. 'I can't believe she's gone … I just can't believe it,' I cried.

Looking up, I saw Gary standing at the living-room door. He knelt down on the floor beside us and the three of us just held one another.

Eventually we got up and went to the living room, where Martin poured each of us a large whisky. Normally I can't stand the stuff but I gulped it down, desperate for anything to take the edge off my pain.

An hour later, we heard a key in the lock and Mum and Dad walked into the room, their faces haggard and strained. They sat down wearily on the sofa, and gratefully took a drink from Martin.

'It was very peaceful in the end,' Dad said quietly. 'She opened her eyes for a few seconds, then she closed them and just slipped away gently. She knew we were with her, and she wasn't in any pain. My wee girl was so brave …'

Dad broke down, and the sight of him so utterly broken after watching his daughter die was horrendous.

The doorbell went, startling us all, and I went to answer it. Katrina, Paul and my other cousin, John, stood on the doorstep. They looked pale and exhausted.

'Can we come in?' asked Katrina.

'Of course,' I said. 'We should all be together tonight.'

The eight of us sat in the living room until the sun rose, remembering Nicole. Sometimes crying, sometimes laughing, trying to take in the fact she was gone.

Just before dawn broke, Paul, Katrina, John and Martin left and we all went to bed, despite knowing sleep would be an impossibility. I climbed into Nicole's bed and gazed at the photo she kept of the two of us on her bedside table. I couldn't believe that my vivacious sister, who was so desperate to live and who could have done so much with her life, was now lying cold in a hospital mortuary, just a few miles from here.

I clenched my fists with rage that she'd been taken away from us.

The birds began to sing outside the window, but their cheery chorus sounded so wrong to my ears. 'There will never be happiness again,' I thought. 'I will never be able to laugh or smile now she's gone.'

As the sun rose and Nicole's room grew bright, I realised today was the beginning of the rest of my life without my twin, and that nothing would ever be the same without her.

Chapter Twelve

The day after Nicole died, Mum, Dad, Gary and I sat around the kitchen table, completely drained and shell-shocked.

The whole house felt hollow and silent without the sound of Nicole's cheeky laugh. The empty chair at the table, where Nicole usually sat, was painful even to look at. There had been so many happy meals, family squabbles and hours spent playing board games around this table.

So many memories … and that's all there would ever be now, because we would never again be a complete family.

We had no future with no Nicole in it, only a past.

We gathered to talk about something no family should ever have to discuss: a sister and daughter's funeral.

I looked at my parents, their hands cupped around the mugs of hot sugary tea which Mum had made for us all, and I barely recognised them. It was as if they had both aged 10 years overnight. Their faces were grey, their eyes glazed, as if something inside them had died with their baby girl.

Gary stared down at the table, his shoulders tense and hunched; I knew he was too scared to make eye contact with any of us in case he broke down.

'I'm going to take care of everything,' I announced. 'I know just how she'd want her funeral to be, and I want to do this for her.'

'No, Melissa. It's too much for you,' said Mum. 'We'll help.'

'Mum, I'm doing this,' I said firmly. 'You and Dad have done enough. Now it's my turn. Let me do this for her.'

They both reached for my hands, nodding gratefully.

'Thank you, Melissa,' Dad said, his usually booming voice now barely a whisper, as if the effort to speak under the weight of his sadness was just too much. 'Thank God we still have you and Gary.'

I'm sure a psychologist would say I used planning Nicole's funeral as a way to keep my own grief at bay; to suspend the reality that she was gone for as long as possible. But the thought of giving her the very best goodbye was all that was keeping me going at that point. The guilt that I had been abroad when she fell ill for the final time, and hadn't been strong enough to stay with her until the very end, was haunting me. Taking care of her funeral would, I hoped, ease it and make me feel I had done enough for her at the end of her life. I knew I was dangerously close to a complete breakdown but I've always been a 'do-er' and having to hold it together to plan Nicole's funeral was what was keeping me from falling into my own abyss of sorrow.

I spent the morning on the phone to the undertakers and the church, and it was decided that her funeral would be held in one week's time, on 19 July, at 11 a.m., at St Constantine's in Govan. It had been our family church all our life. We'd both been baptised there, and we'd made our Communion and then our Confirmation there too. As little girls imagining our wedding days, it had always been this church we thought we'd come to as brides one day. Now Nicole would be going to the church in a coffin instead of a wedding dress, and she would never proudly bring her own babies to be baptised there. Amidst all the happy memories I had from this church, now it would always be the place where I said goodbye to my sister, for ever.

The rest of the week passed by in a flash. There was so much to do, and I relished my long 'To Do' list that helped fill each day and left me so exhausted at night I fell into a deep, dreamless sleep.

My half-sisters Laura and Kelly flew up for the funeral, and stayed at our house.

'I know we can never replace Nicole, but always know that you have two other sisters and we will always be here for you,' said Laura, hugging me tightly when they arrived from the airport in a taxi.

'I remember how excited we were when you and Nicole were born,' said Kelly. 'We were so thrilled to be big sisters, and you two were like our little dolls when we came to visit. I just can't believe she's gone … But there will always be a piece of her here, in you, Melissa. She is a part of you. Don't forget that.'

For the first time in days I smiled – at the thought a little piece of my sister would always be with me.

With such a big extended family, people were queueing up to offer their help in any way they could. And although I wanted to be in charge of all the arrangements, determined to protect Mum and Dad from the pain of planning their own daughter's funeral, I was grateful I could lean on others when I needed to.

Nicole's death certificate had to be collected from the council offices where births, deaths and marriages are recorded, and my cousin John drove me to get it. As I sat waiting in the dreary council office, I thought back to how we had loved to look at our birth certificates when we were small, asking Mum what we were like as babies. Mum and Dad had sat in this very room 21 years ago, to formally register our births, both of them proud as Punch to have two newborn daughters.

Now, here I was collecting the piece of the paper which made it official that Nicole had gone.

On the Monday after Nicole died, I met with the funeral director. It felt completely surreal, in the most awful way possible, to be sat discussing in which coffin my sister should be buried. In fact, I had been feeling physically sick as he showed me a catalogue of coffins – but I suddenly found myself having to stifle a fit of giggles.

'I'm so sorry,' I said to the man, who looked completely bewildered at my sudden change of mood. 'It's just that I'm a notorious shopaholic and I can imagine my sister rolling her eyes at me out shopping for a coffin. She'd have found it really funny that, even now, I'd found an excuse to shop.'

He nodded, professionally, but I'm not sure he understood.

Despite Nicole's positivity about beating cystic fibrosis, there had been times when we'd talked about death. Never really about her dying – I couldn't handle conversations like that – but just death in general. Snippets of those conversations kept flooding back to me now, helping me choose the details of her funeral, and I wondered if Nicole was playing some part in helping me remember those chats, somehow making sure, from wherever she was, that she had the day she wanted.

There were certain details I was absolutely sure about: I knew Nicole wanted a white coffin, and all the flowers had to be yellow, which was one of her favourite colours. 'Yellow's such a happy colour, that's what I'd choose for the church,' she'd told me once. 'I wouldn't want people to wear black, either – it's so miserable. Bright colours only, please. I'd want it to be a celebration.'

'Oh, hush, Nicole,' I'd said. 'This is such a morbid conversation. I'm never going to be arranging your funeral, so there's no point telling me these things. You'll probably outlive me once you get your new lungs.'

Yet here I was, putting her instructions into action, grateful we'd had those conversations so I knew just what she wanted.

Remembering that she wanted only bright colours, with Mum's help I picked out a beautiful emerald-green wrap dress from her wardrobe for her to be buried in. Two months before she died, she'd worn it to our Aunt Carol's sixtieth birthday (Mum's sister-in-law). Even though it had been a huge effort for her to go, because she was so weak and tired so easily, she'd been adamant she wasn't missing it.

Ironing the dress and placing it in a dress carrier to be taken to the funeral home, I remembered how gorgeous she'd looked in it – green the perfect colour for her red hair and porcelain skin.

One thing I definitely wanted Mum's opinion on was the funeral mass. As a Catholic family, it was important that the religious part of the day was done properly, as well as reflecting what Nicole wanted. Each sipping a glass of wine, we sat at the kitchen table poring over a large hymn book and another of readings for funerals. Flicking through the hymn book for inspiration, I came to one in the children's section, which Nicole and I used to sing at school when we were little, called 'If I Were A Butterfly'.

'I think her coffin should be carried in to this one, Mum,' I said. 'It's a happy hymn, and I think it suits the colour scheme she wanted.'

'Yes, I can remember you both as wee nippers singing that. It's perfect,' Mum agreed.

Together we chose two more hymns, 'Here I Am, Lord' and 'Be Not Afraid', which had both been favourites of Nicole's.

'What about at the graveside?' Mum asked. 'We need some music to play there too.'

But I already knew what should be played as Nicole was buried. A few weeks before her death, we'd been driving to the shops when a song came on the car radio. Called 'Let Her Go' by a band called Passenger, it was about how you really only know just how much you love someone once you've let them go.

'I love this song,' Nicole had said to me, singing along to it.

I'd barely paid any attention at the time, but since she'd died that song had been running through my mind day and night, and I knew she'd love to hear it one last time.

By the Wednesday after Nicole's death, the funeral was planned and 250 people had been invited to attend, with strict instructions not to wear black: only bright colours, and preferably yellow.

That evening we had arranged to go and see Nicole's body at the undertakers, where she had been since the weekend. Even though I hadn't been strong enough to stay with her for her death, I was adamant I wanted to see her.

'I need to say goodbye properly,' I told Martin. 'I have to do this.'

However, as we drove up to the entrance of the funeral home, I began to physically shake with nerves. 'I'm not sure I can … maybe this shouldn't be my last memory of her?'

'Melissa, only you know what is right for you,' soothed Mum. 'If it doesn't feel right, don't do it. Nicole will understand.'

I felt completely torn. I wanted to see my sister, kiss her and whisper goodbye to her a final time, but I was terrified she wouldn't look like her any more, that death would have changed her and my last memory of her wouldn't be how I wanted to remember her.

I stood with my hand on the handle of the door leading to where she was laid out in her coffin for what felt like an age.

'Nicole, tell me what to do,' I prayed. 'I just don't know.' Eventually, I let go of the handle and walked away from the door. 'I can't, I just can't,' I said, collapsing into my dad's arms.

'Don't worry, sweetheart,' he said, gently kissing the top of my head. 'There are lots of ways to say goodbye to her. It doesn't have to be here.'

I had brought with me an Eeyore teddy which Nicole had bought me years before. 'I want this to go in her coffin with her,' I said.

'Give it to me, I'll do it,' said Mum, taking it from my arms and walking into the room where Nicole's body lay.

I was wracked with guilt that I wasn't brave enough to go with her but, watching Mum come out of the room, her face pale and puffy from crying, I felt relieved I'd made the decision I had.

'She looks so peaceful,' Mum said, 'but I think that's the hardest thing I've ever had to do, seeing my baby like that. She's so cold and still now, not like my bubbly, vivacious wee girl.'

On Thursday, the day before the funeral, I realised that I'd been so busy planning everything, I hadn't sorted out anything to wear for myself. I rummaged through my wardrobe but nothing I had felt right.

'I'll take you shopping,' Katrina offered, when I phoned to tell her. 'It'll do you good to take a break for a few hours.'

That afternoon we drove into Glasgow's city centre and headed straight for Topshop. I never normally shopped there, but Nicole loved it and I had a strong feeling I'd find the right outfit there.

Walking through the store, suddenly I stopped dead. Hanging on a rail in front of me was the exact same wrap dress Nicole was to be buried in, only this one was in yellow. And the only dress left was in my size.

'It's a sign,' I said to Katrina, taking it from the hanger. 'I can't believe this. It's just perfect. And Nicole would be really flattered I was copying her style!'

When I got home I took the dress from the bag to show Mum, who burst out laughing. 'It's been years since you let me dress you the same!'

I squeezed her hand. 'I think it was meant to be that I found this dress. So we can be the same, one last time,' I said.

That evening, Nicole's body was taken from the funeral home in a hearse to the church, where she would spend the night before her funeral. It stopped outside our house for a few moments, her last visit home. The street was filled with friends, family and neighbours who'd all gathered to pay their respects.

I stood at the kerb with Mum, Dad and Gary – all of us holding hands. Around us, people muttered quiet prayers, or reached out to touch the hearse, saying their own goodbyes to the girl who'd grown up in this street.

I knew that although she would never be back here again, they would never forget her.

The hearse then drove to the church and we followed by car in silence, each of us unable to take our eyes off the white coffin that held Nicole.

At the church, her coffin was placed in front of the altar and the priest said a few prayers over it. I'd worried I wouldn't want to leave her at the church overnight by herself, but as I touched her coffin and whispered goodbye as we left, I felt alright about it. We both knew this church so well, it was so familiar. She would be safe here, amidst the holy statues and the wooden pews we had sat on for mass so many times in our life together.

When we got home from the church, I knew I had one last thing to do to prepare for the funeral the following day: I needed to write the eulogy I was going to give.

It was another of those things Nicole had mentioned she'd like when we'd talked about death, so as terrified as I was about standing up in front of so many people, I knew I had to do it.

When I'd told Mum and Dad they both looked worried. 'Are you sure you're going to be able to get through it?' Dad had asked. 'It will be very difficult, and we don't want you feeling under pressure if you think it will be too upsetting for you.'

'It's what she wanted and I'm not going to let her down,' I replied. 'I can't guarantee there won't be tears, but I'll get to the end somehow.'

When everyone else went to bed that night I sat at the kitchen table with a notepad and pen, and asked Nicole for inspiration: 'Help me find the right words, 'Cole. Help me not mess this up. I want to do you proud,' I whispered out loud.

For the next hour I scribbled notes, crossing out bits I wasn't happy with, underlining the parts I knew would be hardest to get through without breaking down, and practising them over and over in a hushed whisper. Finally, I felt happy with what I'd written and carefully folded the sheet of paper with the eulogy neatly written on it, placing it in my handbag so I didn't forget it.

Crawling into bed, I was exhausted but I couldn't sleep. Something was niggling away at the back of my mind, keeping me awake. Had I forgotten to do something? No, everything had been arranged, every last detail taken care of. So what was it, this overwhelming feeling that there was something important I still had to do for her? Quietly, I crept from my room into Nicole's, hoping that by feeling close to her, I'd realise what it was that was bothering me.

Minutes later, as I sat at her computer, reading and rereading the list of wishes she'd left behind, I knew then what had compelled me to search for this final task, the last thing I could do for her. My skin was covered in goosebumps, and I was convinced that somehow Nicole had made sure I'd found this secret list of hers.

She had been robbed of the chance to fulfil her own wishes, but I instinctively knew she wanted me to do them for her in her memory. 'I'll make your wishes come true, Nicole,' I whispered. 'I'll complete this list for you.'

All week I'd seen her funeral as my final connection with her, but as I crept back to my own room, I realised, with a glint of hope, that a new chapter in our life together was only just beginning.

Chapter Thirteen

The morning of Nicole's funeral dawned and, as I pulled open my bedroom curtains, I smiled a little, relieved to see a perfectly clear blue sky and warm sun over the city. Knowing how much she wanted today to be a celebration, I'd fervently prayed for good weather during the week since her death. Dark clouds and rain just wouldn't have been right on a day when my sister wanted to see smiles, bright colours and for people to remember her with love and laughter, not tears.

I just hoped I was going to be able to hold myself together and give her that day, without breaking down.

I'd barely slept a wink since I'd crept back to my bedroom from hers, after discovering her secret list just hours before. Lying awake, my mind had raced from thought to thought and emotion to emotion. I'd imagined Nicole sitting up late in her room, typing the list, determined that her life after a transplant would be so dramatically different to her life before. Did she smile as she typed it? Did she giggle as she dreamt up some of the funny ones, like, 'Fart in a lift' and 'Go skinny-dipping'? Had she become emotional, imagining herself fit and well, climbing the Eiffel Tower?

I wondered when she would have told me about it, and would she have asked me to join her in doing some of the wishes? I felt sure she would have. When she became very unwell, before I made it home from Spain, did she know she was going to die and did she wonder what would become of her list? I hoped so much she trusted our twin bond would guide me to it.

The same mix of emotions continued to surge through me that I'd felt the night before – the anger she hadn't been able to make her own dreams come true, but at the same time a deep-rooted resolve in my heart that I would do it all for her.

As I showered and dried my hair, I thought about whether to tell anyone else yet. For these last few hours, it had been mine and Nicole's little secret, but I knew it couldn't stay that way. And while I loved having this final bond with her, I wanted to share it with everyone else who loved her too. I knew it would mean so much to them, and I also knew I was going to need all the help I could get to complete her list. If I'm honest, I was beginning to feel a bit daunted at how much there was to do. I wanted to fulfil the list right down to the last, smallest wish. I decided to tell just Mum, Dad, Gary, Laura and Kelly that morning, hoping it would lift their spirits a bit and help them through the day ahead. There would be plenty of time in the days and weeks ahead to tell other people.

Over breakfast, I shared the news of my discovery with them, putting the list, which I'd printed off from Nicole's laptop, on the table. Their faces revealed the same spectrum of emotions I had experienced myself: shock, sadness, but also happiness that we still had this last piece of Nicole to hold on to. Mum, Dad and Gary were speechless, and I could see each of them struggling with the thought that Nicole had been robbed of so many dreams by her death.

It was Laura who spoke first, making the wonderful suggestion that she and Kelly begin the list by buying Nicole a pair of shoes costing over £100.

'Why don't we go and get her a pair of shoes this morning, and she can wear them today?' asked Laura.

'Yeah. That way we can do something to help you complete the list and Nicole will get to wear a really special pair of heels for her funeral,' said Kelly.

For a split second, I felt a flash of protectiveness over the list, and wondered if maybe I should refuse their offer and fulfil every wish by myself. But almost immediately I realised that Nicole would have wanted me to include all the people she loved, whenever I had the opportunity. We had always thought our older sisters were so glamorous and sophisticated, so it felt right that they help with this particular wish. Family and friends had been so important to Nicole – she was happiest surrounded by them, as if their love helped to distract her from her illness. And this was just one wish out of a long list – there would be plenty more for me to do alone.

'That's a brilliant idea,' I said. 'Nicole would be tickled pink to think she was going to her funeral in a pair of expensive shoes. Let's do it!'

As they sped off in Dad's car to the shops, I went back upstairs to get dressed. I carefully applied my make-up and did my hair before slipping on the yellow dress I'd bought for the funeral, teaming it with a pair of wedges that Nicole had bought me for my holiday to Spain just two weeks before.

It felt like years, not weeks, since she had presented me with a shoebox as I had been packing my case the night before I left.

'Here's a wee holiday present for you,' she'd said. 'I ordered them online for you, and they arrived this morning. I hope you like them.'

'Oh, Nicole, you didn't need to do that!' I replied. 'But they're absolutely gorgeous. Thank you!'

I'd hugged her, wincing as she went into a coughing spasm, her body so fragile and light in my arms.

Had it really only been a fortnight since Nicole had stood here in my bedroom with me, watching me try on these shoes? Two weeks since I had still had my twin, and my heart didn't ache permanently with the pain of missing her? Already it felt so long ago since I'd heard her voice or snuggled up beside her on the sofa for a gossip.

I suddenly felt scared about the years that lay ahead without her. Would I forget that her hair smelled of apricot-scented shampoo when I brushed it for her, or that she loved ribs, or the sound of her mischievous laugh as she watched one of her favourite DVDs? I didn't want to forget any of the little things about her that had made Nicole who she was.

My whole life lay ahead of me, but now there would be so many milestones that she wouldn't be a part of. If Martin and I got married, she wouldn't be my bridesmaid and help me plan the day. She'd never be godmum to my children, who'd call her Auntie 'Cole and beg to have sleepovers at her house, which would be just around the corner from mine. We would never be old ladies together, going for afternoon tea in posh hotels, still inseparable despite our years.

I sat down on my bed and buried my face in my hands. 'Nicole, please come back,' I said out loud. 'How can I live my life without you in it? It wasn't meant to be like this …' I sat for a few minutes, taking deep breaths and gathering myself. 'Come on, Melissa,' I said to myself sternly. 'Pull yourself together. Nicole needs you to be strong today.'

Standing up, I adjusted my dress in the mirror and held my head high. Now wasn't the time to think about the future. There was a funeral to get through, and I wasn't going to let my sister down.

Downstairs, Laura and Kelly had arrived back, flushed from their speedy dash to the shops. I gasped with delight as Laura gently lifted the shoes from their box – a pair of very high, peep-toe, fuchsia-pink strappy heels decorated with diamantes so they caught the light. They were so glitzy, and I could just see Nicole in them. The price tag of £110 was still stuck to the bottom of one of them, and I peeled it off, mentally ticking off the first wish from my sister's list.

'They're perfect,' I said, putting my arms around both girls. 'She'd love them.' As we hugged each other tightly in the middle of the kitchen, the three of us wept. These beautiful shoes would only be worn once, to a funeral: never to a disco, or on a romantic dinner date with a boyfriend. Nicole would never totter in on them in the early hours after a night on the tiles, and we'd never squabble over whether I could borrow them.

As Laura and Kelly jumped in the car again to drive to the church and place them in Nicole's coffin, I felt that beginning the list then was a good omen. While the day was about saying goodbye and marking the end of Nicole's life, the list was just beginning – the start of something so incredibly important to her, and now to me, too. By beginning it on today of all days, it helped me feel there was a balance – a feeling of hope and looking forward, as well as the desperate sadness of knowing I was never going to see my sister again.

Martin was sitting at the kitchen table in his suit, his tea and toast untouched in front of him. I knew how hard it was for him, trying to support me while grieving for Nicole too.

'Are you OK?' he asked, as I sipped a glass of water, my stomach too nervous to even contemplate eating breakfast.

'Sort of …' I replied. Standing up, he pulled me into his arms and hugged me tightly. I rested my head on his shoulder, breathing in his familiar scent of soap and aftershave. 'I'm so glad I have you, Martin,' I whispered in his ear. 'I honestly couldn't get through this without you.'

'You'll always have me,' he replied. 'Always. And I'm so incredibly proud of you and how you've sorted everything out for today.'

By 10.30 a.m. we were ready to leave for the church. The atmosphere in the house changed from one of busyness and chaos to nervousness. Each of us was quiet, mentally preparing for what was ahead.

Our final hours with Nicole.

'Is everyone ready?' Dad asked, nervously adjusting his tie. He rarely wore a suit and it was strange seeing him so smartly dressed and clearly uncomfortable. We all nodded. 'Come on, then. Let's go and give our beautiful girl the send-off she deserves,' he said. 'Today's going to be so hard, but we'll get through it together.'

And with those words we walked out through the front door, towards the black funeral car which sat at the kerb to take us to the church, where Nicole was waiting for us.

Chapter Fourteen

The last few mourners were hurrying into the church as our car pulled up outside. I smiled with relief when I saw they had come wearing bright colours, as we'd requested. I'd worried some people might think it strange to request they didn't wear black, as if we weren't taking the fact this was a funeral seriously. To see they had got into the spirit of celebration we wanted for today was a relief.

We entered the church as a group and walked to the front, past the pews filled with friends and family who had travelled from all over Scotland, England and beyond to be with us. I just hoped Nicole knew how loved she was, that so many people had come so far, to say goodbye to her. She'd always adored being the centre of attention, so it was incredibly bittersweet she was centre-stage today for the most tragic of reasons.

'All these people should be gathered here to see her married, or attend her child's baptism, not to see her buried,' I thought sadly, as I took my seat at the front of the church beside Martin.

The church was filled with flowers and their sweet aroma filled the air, lifting my spirits a little. There were roses, sunflowers and tiny buttercups in huge arrangements on the altar, so vibrant and colourful. I knew they were just what Nicole would have chosen.

At the front of the church, in front of the altar where the priest would stand and say mass, was Nicole's coffin. A shaft of light fell on it through one of the stained-glass windows, bathing it in warm summer sunshine and colour. I couldn't take my eyes off it. It was so hard to believe Nicole was in there, just yards from me, and yet I would never see her face again. Even though she had been dead for a week, I still hadn't been able to get my head around that fact. Part of me kept expecting her to pop her head around my bedroom door to say hello, or to hear her laughing as she played with her two dogs.

When you've been with someone for over 21 years, as we had, seeing them almost every single day and feeling like they are the other half of you, the thought of them not being there any more is just so hard to comprehend.

The organ began playing, jolting me from my private thoughts, and we stood in unison for the first hymn, 'If I Were A Butterfly'. I glanced over at Mum as we sang and she nodded to me. It had been the right choice, this happy and childlike hymn. 'I'd thank you Lord for giving me wings . .' Yes, it was a painful reminder that this was the funeral of someone who had been far too young to die, but it was setting the right tone that this would be a celebration.

The funeral mass went by so quickly, filled with prayers for Nicole and more hymns. At times I could hear the sound of people crying quietly, but when the priest, Father McCann, who had known Nicole and me since we were seven years old, spoke about her, there was also fond laughter as he recalled the little red-headed girl with the cheeky smile coming up the aisle to make her First Communion all those years ago.

The familiarity of the mass was comforting and I silently offered up my own prayers that wherever she was, Nicole was happy and not in pain anymore.

Before I knew it, the time had come for me to read my eulogy. As I stood up my heart was racing and my palms were sweaty.

'Good luck,' Martin whispered. 'You can do this.'

I walked up to the very front of the church and into the pulpit. Looking out at the sea of faces, most of them so familiar to me, I felt my knees knocking together. Taking a deep breath, I began to speak into the microphone: 'We've come together here today to remember Nicole. To some of you she was a daughter, a niece or a cousin, to others a friend or a pupil. She was my sister but she was also much, much more than that … she was the other half of me.' I stopped. Taking a moment, I inhaled deeply, trying to get my emotions under control. I glanced over at Mum and Dad, both of them silently weeping, and immediately looked away before I broke down too. 'Today I stand in front of you as the proudest twin sister in the world, and it's an honour to share with you all some of my memories of Nicole. Although I was nine minutes older than Nicole, she was always the leader out of the two of us; the brave twin who wasn't afraid of anything. I looked up to her, and she inspired me every single day with how she remained so positive and so determined to live life to the fullest in the face of so much pain and suffering.' I smiled a little, remembering so vividly this aspect of Nicole. '"Double trouble" is often how Nicole and I were described and I think that's fair. From escaping from our playpen to covering the kitchen and ourselves in butter one day when Mum had her back turned, we were never far from mischief as little girls.' I looked up, happy to hear the gentle, affectionate laughter of everyone. 'Nicole loved to perform and show off – many of you will have seen the singing and dancing performances she used to put on in the living room, or the catwalk shows she did, wobbling around in Mum's high heels. Nicole grew into a beautiful teenager and young woman, but cystic fibrosis grew with her. She battled hard against the disease, never losing her kind, funny personality even when she was being denied a normal life.' I looked up again at the congregation, which was nodding in agreement. 'Nicole had everyone she knew wrapped around her little finger, me included. Whatever she wanted, from a milkshake from McDonald's to one of her favourite cupcakes from the local bakery, or the latest DVD release, there was always a friend or family member there to get it for her when she wasn't well enough to go herself. And in return she gave us all so much love and laughter. I'd have done anything for her. I just wish I'd been able to do more to keep her with us …'

Me (on the right) and Nicole, aged one, all dressed up in our Scottish outfits! I love Nicole's cheeky grin.

Once again in matching outfits, on a family day out to Largs, North Ayrshire.

Visiting the neighbours at our childhood home in Langcroft Place, Shieldhall, with our brother Gary. Notice we're all wearing the same shoes, even if he managed to avoid the matching dresses!

Our photo at St Jerome's Primary School in Govan, when Nicole and I were seven and Gary was six. Three peas in a pod.

Nicole loved performing and showing off! She used to sing for us in the living room or do catwalk shows in Mum's high heels. In this photo she's roped me in on the mic, too.

At our First Holy Communion with Gran Tennant and Nana Cauley. We were so excited to have our dresses made by a real dressmaker – we felt like princesses!

Nicole won a competition in a newspaper when she was 13 years old to be a flag bearer for the Celtic player, Henrik Larsson. I felt so proud watching her on TV, lining up in front of thousands of people, a massive grin on her face.

At our 12th birthday party, posing with our cake in front of the poster of Lubo Moravcik (a player from Nicole's football team, Celtic).

I felt the wind had been knocked out of me the first time I saw Nicole in a wheelchair. She became so breathless at times that she couldn't walk to the end of the street, and the oxygen tank went with her everywhere. I found it so hard to watch, but she was so brave.

At our 18th birthday party, which Nicole decided was to be fancy dress. She went as Poison Ivy from the Batman films, so I continued her theme and went as The Riddler.

My beautiful sister Nicole. She was so happy that night, dancing with all her friends, singing along to her favourite songs.

At our 21st party with Mum and Dad. Three years on was such a contrast – Nicole was hardly able to dance, sitting hunched and swollen in her wheelchair for most of the night. But there was still a twinkle in her eye.

Thanks to Nicole's bucket list, which I vowed to complete for her, I'm now a bona fide world record breaker! I couldn't have done it without my friends and family. We made quite the roller conga team.

A group trip to The Stand Comedy Club, in Glasgow's West End, somewhere Nicole always wanted to go. Left to right is Martin, Katrina, Paul, me, Joanne, Uncle John and Alana.

Nicole was always celeb-mad, so I know this was one of the wishes she most wanted to fulfil. I was so lucky to meet the *Strictly Come Dancing 2014* stars, and even managed to get photos with a few of my favourites. Here I am with Mark Wright!

Mum and I climbed all 704 steps of the Eiffel Tower!

I was a natural when I tried out archery and shooting, as per Nicole's list. I know why she wished she'd had a chance to try them – what a great way of letting off steam!

I can't believe I posed nude in front of all these people! I bet you were having a proper laugh at the idea of this art class, Nicole.

One of the more exotic wishes – riding a camel in Lanzarote. I think you thought it would make you feel like an Arabian princess, but the reality was much smellier …

I never wanted a tattoo, but when I saw it on Nicole's list, I knew it was time. She'll always be a part of me, but now it's there for everyone to see.

The words from the E. E. Cummings' poem, 'Dive for Dreams', that meant so much to us, now inked on me forever.

With my husband to be! Wasn't sure how I'd make the wish to 'get married' come true, but luckily Martin stepped in to help me out. And I know you can't be there in body, 'Cole, but I hope you'll be there as my maid of honour in spirit. I'll love you forever, my special twin.

Glancing over at Martin, he smiled and winked, and I knew he was willing me on, to find the strength to finish my tribute. 'Nicole used to talk about death sometimes, but I hoped this day would be many, many years away. We all did,' I added. 'I don't want to say goodbye to her today – none of us do. We have to, but before we do I'll leave you with one last memory of my sister. When Nicole and I were younger, and she used to spend time in hospital, she would call home to say goodnight to me every night. At the end of every call we would sing a little song to one another that we'd made up, about how we'd never, ever be apart from one another.' I took a deep breath, ready now to draw to a close this tribute to my sister. 'And, in fact, a piece of her *will* always be here; in me, in our family, and in each of you who knew her. And so, as incredibly painful as it is to say goodbye to her today, in a way she will never be apart from us.'

With those final words, I broke down.

It was as if all the grief I'd been bottling up for the past week since her death, focusing on the funeral arrangements, was flooding out of me. Blinded by tears, I stumbled from the pulpit and shakily walked back to my seat. I sat down beside Mum, trembling with sheer relief that I'd got through it. 'That was so hard,' I sobbed, burying my face in her shoulder.

'Well done, Melissa,' she said. 'You did her proud. You did us all proud.'

The mass ended and it was time for Nicole's coffin to be carried from the church. Dad, Gary, Martin, her old boyfriend

Craig, and our cousins Paul and John lifted the coffin and placed it on their shoulders. Many people had offered to carry her coffin, but these six men had been chosen specially, all of us knowing they were who Nicole would have wanted. Tears streamed down their faces as they slowly walked down the aisle of the church. It hurt to see these normally strong men so broken by their grief, and the knowledge they were carrying Nicole on her final journey. Each of them had their own precious memories of her, as a daughter and a sister, a friend, a girlfriend, a cousin. And, like for me, none of their lives would now be the same without her.

I walked behind the coffin, arm in arm with Mum; we were supporting one another physically and emotionally.

'It was just what she would have wanted, Melissa. Thank you,' Mum whispered to me as we passed the packed rows of mourners, and I felt some sense of satisfaction and relief that my planning had come together, and that Nicole would be happy with how her day had gone.

Nicole's coffin was gently placed in the back of a hearse and we climbed into the funeral car for the short journey to the cemetery. We were all quiet, lost in our own thoughts. I stared out of the window, watching the people out and about on the streets doing their shopping, buying lunch and hurrying in and out of offices. It was so strange to see that the world outside our family was carrying on as normal. For us, life had ground to a halt, and there would be no such thing as normality any more.

I envied those people smiling in the sunshine. Just a few weeks ago, I had been one of them, planning my holiday and looking forward to some time off work, but now it felt like that Melissa was another person. So much had changed since then, which could never be unchanged.

At the graveyard, the same six men carried Nicole's coffin to the freshly-dug grave, which was surrounded by mourners. We'd decided not to have a private burial. We knew it was important to so many people to pay their respects at her graveside, and we didn't want to deny them that.

Rather than bury Nicole in a new plot, it had been decided she'd be buried beside our uncle, Joe, who'd died the year before. We hadn't wanted her to be alone, the thought of placing her into the cold ground difficult enough.

Gary had hooked his iPod up to a speaker and, as the pristine white coffin was slowly lowered into the grave, the song 'Let Her Go' by Passenger played.

Some people had brought single yellow roses and they dropped them on top of the coffin as the priest said a final prayer over it.

I clung to Martin as I listened to the lyrics of the music, which seemed like they had been written for this moment. How sometimes we only truly appreciate the one we loved so much when we lose them: 'You only miss the sun when it starts to snow'.

As a final tribute to Nicole, our cousins Dianne and Christine had arranged for 21 bright yellow balloons to be brought to the graveside so we could release them into the summer sky, one for each year of her life.

The three of us, and Katrina, released them as the music played. They sailed up high into the sky until they were just tiny yellow specks against the stunning blue sky, which reminded me of Nicole's eyes.

'Fly high, Nicole,' I thought to myself. 'No more pain, no more medicine, no more hospitals ... you're free from all that now.'

As the grave was filled with earth, and her flower-strewn coffin was lost from view, people began to drift away to their cars. I stood alone for a few moments, unable to tear myself away from her. 'I hope today's been everything you would have wanted, 'Cole,' I whispered softly. 'I'm not going to say goodbye just yet, though. Not until I've completed every one of your wishes. Wish me luck, sis. I know you'll be watching over me.'

PART TWO

PART TWO

Letter One
July 2013

Dear 'Cole,

It feels so strange to be writing to you, instead of just being able to talk to you. It's just after midnight and I'm snuggled up in your bed to feel close to you, with LouLou and Ralph sleeping at my feet. I can still smell your DKNY perfume on the sheets, and there's a neatly folded pile of your clothes sitting on the dressing table, just waiting for you to put them away. Your room is just as it was the day you died, only a few short weeks ago – nothing has been touched. Even your hair extensions are still hanging over your chair, where you must have tossed them. I know you wore them to hide your hair loss but I thought you were beautiful with or without them.

It really feels like you could walk in the door any second. But I know you won't.

The pain is still so raw – none of us has the emotional strength to do anything but come to this room to feel close to you. I can't ever imagine us packing up all your DVDs and books, taking your pictures down from the walls and making this nothing more than a spare bedroom. It's *your* room, Nicole, and it will never be anything else in my mind.

All the times we lay here on your bed together, gossiping for hours, or the countless times a day I'd pick up the phone at work and call you for a chat about nothing at all … I realise now I took it for granted.

I'd give *anything* to do that now, just to hear your voice even one last time, but I can't. You're gone, and I don't know where you are, but I'll place this letter in the memory box I've started for you, and hope you'll be able to read it somehow.

I've started it, Nicole – your list. It's underway. I know you used to tease me for being the more organised, conscientious twin (or, in your words, the 'geeky' one) but even by my standards I'm feeling pretty proud I've got it off the ground already.

The last few weeks have passed in a blur. Dad and I both went back to work a few days after your funeral. I'm sure some people thought it was too soon but we both needed to get back into a routine. Sitting at home wasn't helping us and I suppose for me it was a way to pretend everything was still normal, even though I knew it wasn't.

At first I wasn't spending much time at home – it was too hard to be here without you. If I wasn't working, I'd go to Martin's or a friend's; anything but come home to the constant reminders that you weren't there anymore.

Mum has barely left the house this month. She's not back at work yet, and when she's not sitting with the steady stream of visitors to the house, she just seems lost. She sits here in your room and she cries – her heart is completely broken, Nicole. You and she were together so much, almost as much as we were. Without you to care for, worry about and fuss over, I know she feels her life has lost meaning: since the day you were diagnosed, so much of her life focused on you. I find it so hard to see her like this, but what can I say or do to make it better? And even though I'm getting up for work in the morning, doing my job, seeing friends and seem to be functioning, inside, I'm just as lost as she is.

I know you didn't plan for me to do the list, that it was meant to be *yours* to complete, once you'd had your transplant, but I'm so grateful you left this piece of you behind. Already I realise how much I'm going to need it to distract me from missing you. I miss you so much it hurts.

I need something to focus on, something positive, and the list is it.

'Spend Over £100 On Shoes'

Your first wish was fulfilled just seven days after you died, Nicole. When I first read the list, I wasn't surprised to see this wish on it. Being unable to work, you couldn't afford the expensive pairs of shoes you saw in fancy shop windows, but I know your plan was to get a really good job after you had your transplant, save up and splurge on a really amazing pair of heels.

Everyone knew how much you loved your fancy shoes – you'd spend hours poring over images of designer pairs in magazines, like the red-soled Christian Louboutins, tearing them out and sticking them into a scrapbook.

'One day, La La – one day I'll have a house with a walk-in closet, just like in the *Sex And The City* movie, and I'll fill it with expensive shoes,' you'd sigh wistfully. 'And I'll always be able to get them in my size.'

So, we did it for you, Nicole.

You had such tiny feet, didn't you? Only a size one, and it wasn't always easy for you to find the latest styles of shoes in your size. Often we'd come home empty-handed and disappointed after going shoe shopping for you, so when you did find a pair in your size you treasured them. Even when you weren't well enough to go out to bars and clubs, you'd insist on wearing a pair of sparkly stilettos around the house with your jammies.

'The living room is my catwalk,' you'd joke, doing a twirl for us all and flicking your hair back like a proper diva.

All through your funeral mass, when I was desperately trying to hold it together and not completely fall apart, I thought about you dancing and twirling around in your shoes. Ever since we were little girls you loved to dance, didn't you? Whether it was in the kitchen to pop songs on the radio, or on the rare occasions when we were older, and you were well enough to go clubbing with me.

Now you can dance for ever, Nicole, with no breathlessness or pain to stop you, in the shoes of your dreams.

'Get 10 People To Sign Up For Donor Cards'

As you were stuck at home so much, we were always so aware how your laptop was your connection to the outside world, Nicole. You'd spend hours on forums for people with cystic fibrosis and on social media sites like Facebook. I know it helped you feel more 'normal', being in touch with other people your age who were going through the same things as you, and who could really understand how you were feeling. We all tried our best but I know we could never fully comprehend how hard life was for you at times.

These online friends from all over the UK – most of whom you'd never met, could never meet – I never felt jealous of the connection you had with them. I was just grateful you had people out there who could give you advice and support when I didn't know how to help you.

After you died, I took your place on these forums and sites, and had the awful job of telling people you were gone. You'd been in their position several times, when you'd lost friends with cystic fibrosis – like your close friend, Gaynor. But telling people you had died was horrendous. Tears had rolled down my face as I typed the words with shaking hands. 'Hello, everyone. This is Melissa, Nicole's twin sister. I'm so sorry to have to tell you all this, but my sister has died …'

Within minutes your Facebook page was inundated with messages from guys and girls, all devastated to hear you'd lost your battle with cystic fibrosis.

You were so loved, Nicole, even by people you'd never met. They sensed your specialness even from hundreds of miles away, through a computer.

'If there's anything we can do to help your family get through this time, just let us know,' one of the messages read.

And it was then that I thought of something: your wish for people to sign up to the Organ Donor Register.

You always said that if more people signed up there would be more organs available for transplants, and that would mean it wouldn't be as tough for people like you to qualify for a transplant. And also that once someone made it on to the list, the wait wouldn't be as long.

You knew better than anyone that so many people died because they didn't meet the very strict criteria for transplant or because they were stuck on the list, waiting and waiting for an organ because there was such a shortage. You never even made it on to the transplant list, but maybe if there had been more organs available you'd have got on to it, and your life might have been saved.

It used to make you so angry that more people weren't signed up to be organ donors: 'It's so selfish. It just takes a few moments and it could save so many lives. I don't understand what's stopping people,' you'd rage. 'No one needs their organs when they're dead, so why not give someone else a chance at a normal life? If I was well, and was allowed to sign up, I'd do it in a heartbeat!'

Of all your wishes, Nicole, this one has made the most sense to me because I know it must have been one of the most important to you. And I knew it would be an amazing legacy to you knowing that your death had inspired even just 10 people to take those few moments and sign up.

So, the week after you died, I posted a message on Facebook and on all forums of which you were a member: 'For anyone who'd like to do something in Nicole's memory, please either sign up to the NHS Organ Donor Register or, if you already have, then encourage at least one person you know to do it.'

Nicole, your wish was for 10 people to sign up. In fact, hundreds have. In your memory.

I've had messages and texts and emails from friends, family and perfect strangers who saw the request and carried out your wish. Isn't that amazing? I know it's too late for you, and nothing is going to bring you back to us, but I'm sure this means lives are going to be saved.

And thanks, to your list, it's not just human lives which are going to be saved, either.

'Save A Life'

When I read this one I wasn't at all sure how I was going to make it come true for you. 'How on earth do you save a life?' I wondered. Should I start hanging around the local swimming pool in case someone almost drowned? Or cruise the motorways of Scotland waiting to save a crash victim from their wreckage?

Yesterday I had a brainwave. I realised I'd been thinking about this one too literally, and that there were lots of ways to save lives apart from the obvious ones.

'I'm going to donate blood,' I announced to Mum, Dad and Gary. 'That saves lives, doesn't it?'

Simultaneously, they all burst out laughing at me. Can you believe that? Rude, eh!

'Melissa, love, it's a great idea, but have you forgotten you're terrified of needles?' Mum chuckled.

She was right. I even hated watching you inject yourself with your insulin, didn't I? It made me feel a bit queasy and I was in awe at how you didn't even flinch.

'I know, I know,' I replied. 'But if I can't find the courage to do it for Nicole, after all she went through, then I'll be ashamed of myself. I *will* do this, just you wait and see.'

Off I went the next day to a blood donor centre in Glasgow, along with Paul's girlfriend, Alana, who came along to give me some moral support – and pick me off the floor when I saw the needle! Since you died, Nicole, I've grown close to her. Do you remember her? She's been so kind and supportive, despite not knowing you very well.

I'd love to be able to tell you it all went smoothly, but it was a bit of a disaster. After answering a questionnaire about my general health, I had to be weighed as you have to be over a certain weight to give blood.

The scales read just seven stone and two pounds.

'I'm so sorry,' the nurse said, 'but you won't be allowed to give blood at that weight. You have to be over eight stone. Come back when you're a bit heavier.'

We were both always petite, weren't we? But I was really stunned to find out I weighed so little. I think I've definitely lost weight since you died. When I'm sad or stressed I don't have much of an appetite and I've probably been neglecting myself in the last few weeks. And it seems so ironic to me that you battled hard to increase your weight to qualify for a transplant and now I need to do the same, too.

Alana and I left the blood centre, and I was furious that what I'd thought was the perfect way to fulfil your wish had failed.

Stomping down the street in a huff, I looked up and saw a lady collecting for the Dogs Trust. It was definitely one of those eureka moments!

'Nicole never said it had to be a human life. I could save animals instead!' I said to Alana, elated at this new solution.

'That's a great idea,' she replied. 'Nicole was such an animal lover, it's perfect.'

Do you remember the succession of goldfish and budgies you had, growing up? But it was when your Westie, LouLou, was given to you by Mum and Dad, when you were 15, and when Ralph came along a year later, that you were besotted.

They were your constant companions – ones who didn't care if you stayed in your pyjamas all day or had to trail your oxygen tank around the house. They made you laugh, snuggled up to you when they sensed you were feeling down, and followed you everywhere you went. You hated any sort of cruelty to animals, didn't you? And you just couldn't understand how anyone could abuse or neglect them.

'I'm going to set up a monthly donation to the Dogs Trust in Nicole's memory,' I told Alana there and then. 'Think of all the dogs that will help and save. She'd love it.'

So, that's what I've done, Nicole. Every month, a small donation goes to the charity and so, thanks to you, lots of dogs out there are safe and well looked after.

I'm determined I *will* give blood though, just as soon as I weigh enough, so watch this space …

A last note on LouLou and Ralph … they miss you so much – they've not been the same since you died. But we all give them lots of cuddles and treats, spoiling them just like you used to. I'm going to sleep in your bed tonight, Nicole. Me, LouLou and Ralph. We all feel closest to you here in your room.

Sleep tight, sis, wherever you are.

Love,

La La xxx

Letter Two
September 2013

Dear 'Cole,

It's me again, and I've so much to tell you I hardly know where to start.

I laughed out loud when I read the next two wishes on your list, sis: 'Go To A Gay Bar' and 'Have A Dance-off'. That's just you all over, Nicole. In among the really emotional and meaningful wishes, there are the crazily fun ones, like these. You were always the life and soul of any party!

I know it got you down that you couldn't get out more, and I felt so guilty every time I got dressed up for a night out and you couldn't come along. In fact, my favourite nights weren't the ones when I went to posh bars, or danced all night in a club; they were the ones spent at home with you when we'd have our own girls' nights in, just the two of us. Remember how you'd put on all your cheesy Westlife and McFly CDs and we'd dance like loons in the kitchen, sipping bottles of alcopops? We were both complete lightweights and it didn't take much to get us tipsy and giggly. We'd do each other's hair and make-up, then laugh because we looked so glam from the neck up, but just had our pyjamas and slippers on!

But I know you hoped that one day you'd be well enough to have proper nights out, and I wasn't surprised a gay bar would have been your first stop. You loved the gay scene and had lots of gay friends, boys and girls. And I understand exactly why. Like you, they had grown up feeling 'different' to everybody else, and often on the outside of life. You knew exactly how that felt. All your life, all you ever wanted was to be the same and fit in, but your cystic fibrosis always got in the way. People stared at you when you were out in your wheelchair, you missed parties and, stuck indoors or in hospital for months and months, you found it hard to hold on to friendships as people drifted away from you, caught up in their own lives.

Because of this, you never judged or criticised anyone; you just accepted them for who they were. What was it you used to say all the time? 'You are what you are.' And because of that attitude, gay people seemed to gravitate towards you, obviously sensing that with you they would find only fun and friendship, never judgement or condemnation. And, let's be honest, Nicole, you also loved the flamboyance and fun of the gay scene. You were such a drama queen, who loved anything over the top and fabulous!

Fulfilling your next two wishes happened a bit accidentally, in fact.

'Go To A Gay Bar' and 'Have A Dance-off'

I hadn't even been planning to go out – your death is still so recent, and I'm still too deep into trying to come to terms with losing you to even contemplate socialising. But last night Katrina and Paul arrived at the house.

'We're going to a friend's thirtieth birthday party and you're coming with us,' Katrina said.

'No, I'm not,' I replied. 'I don't want to go anywhere. It's too soon.'

'Come on, Melissa, it'll do you good. Nicole wouldn't want you to cut yourself off like this,' said Paul. 'She'd have been the first to say you have to dust yourself off and get on with your life.'

I knew he was right. You more than anyone would have been cross to see me hide away, lost in my grief, wouldn't you?

'OK, OK. I'll come but I'm not staying out late,' I replied, heading upstairs to get changed while they waited for me.

'Don't worry about finding something to wear,' Katrina called after me. 'I've got your outfit in the car.'

'What are you on about?' I asked, turning around, noticing the cheeky smile on her face.

'It's a fancy-dress party and you're going as one of the Pink Ladies with some of the other girls. I'm going to be Jennifer Beals from *Flashdance* and Paul's going as Danny from *Grease*. I've got costumes for us all!'

I burst out laughing. 'You two are crazy! Nicole will be having a right laugh at me going out dressed up like Frenchie!'

At the party, I bumped into an old friend called Keir, who worked as a DJ in local nightclubs. 'I've heard about the list of wishes you're doing for Nicole,' he said. 'I think it's an amazing thing to do for her.' And then he went on, 'I DJ in a gay club in town, and I'm working later on tonight. Do you fancy coming along? I'll make sure you get a table and have a great night.'

At first I wasn't sure. It felt enough just to be out at a party – was I really ready to be out clubbing so soon after your death?

I went to find Katrina and Paul and told them what had just happened.

'We're going,' said Katrina firmly. 'This is the perfect opportunity to fulfil another wish. Nicole always seized the moment, so we will too.'

As you know, Nicole, when Katrina has her mind made up about something there's no point in arguing with her. 'Well, in that case, it looks like we're going to a gay bar!' I smiled.

Me, Katrina and Auntie Fiona all piled into a taxi to a club called AXM, all of us in fancy dress and a bit tipsy already. Before I knew it, we were being ushered to a table in the roped-off VIP area.

'Oh, my God, Nicole would be so jealous,' I said, as a complimentary bottle of champagne was brought to our table.

Trying to be subtle, I peeked over at who was at the table next to us. Guess what! There was Nikki Grahame from *Big Brother*, Lloyd Daniels from *The X Factor* and Benedict Garrett from *Big Brother*!

'Nicole would have loved this!' I shouted to Katrina over the Steps track that was blasting out from the DJ booth. 'She'd have been in her element here!'

And you would have been. The dancefloor was packed, the DJ played all your favourite camper-than-camp pop songs and at one point I looked across the table and Auntie Fiona was getting chatted up by a drag queen! I wish so *so* much we'd gone to a gay club when you were alive. Why didn't we realise our time together was going to be so short? We could have packed so much more in if only we'd known.

A bit later I remembered that you'd also wanted to have a dance-off. 'Katrina, help me find someone to have a dance-off with!' I shouted over the music. 'I'm definitely tipsy enough to not care that I'm a terrible dancer!'

We scoured the dancefloor and eventually settled on Benedict Garrett.

I don't think you'd have believed it was me, Nicole, dancing away in the middle of the floor to Madonna's 'Express Yourself'. Maybe it was the champagne, maybe I was channelling your I-don't-give-a-damn-what-people-think-of-me attitude that I always envied – whatever it was, I danced my heart out for you, giggling away as Benedict even stripped down to his boxers and gyrated around me.

Afterwards we all piled into a taxi and headed back to Auntie Fiona's for a nightcap – not that we needed one. I was on such a high that I'd fulfilled two more of your wishes. But when I walked into Auntie Fiona's kitchen and saw a beautiful photo of you in a frame on the counter, I stopped dead. Suddenly I was crying uncontrollably, Katrina and Auntie Fiona rushing to hold me as I sobbed.

'She should have been here with us tonight. It should have been her on that dancefloor, not me. Why did this have to happen?' I wept. 'I just want her to come back.'

I only wanted to go to bed after that, Nicole, so I called a taxi to take me home.

I crept into your bed, hugging one of your teddies as more tears fell.

Falling apart like that has made me worry. Am I going to be strong enough to do this list for you? Is every wish going to be a painful reminder that you're not here to do it yourself, and am I going to be able to cope with that pain?

I must have drifted off to sleep eventually, as I dreamed of you all night – that you were back here with me.

I woke this morning feeling more positive, though (along with suffering from a champagne headache, of course). Look at everything *you* coped with. You were so strong, right until the end. How dare I be so selfish to think it's going to be too painful to carry out your wishes? Yes, there are times it's going to be hard to do this for you, but nothing is going to stop me.

If the tables were turned, you'd do the same for me. I know that. I won't stop until I've finished every one of your wishes.

And I chalked up another last week, by the way.

'Break A World Record'

Thanks to your list, Nicole, I'm now a bona fide record breaker!

You never wanted to be mediocre so I wasn't surprised to see this wish; I can just imagine how much you'd have boasted about being the best in the world at something. We'd never have heard the end of it!

I hadn't expected to be able to tick this one off your list so quickly, though – I'd anticipated it being one of the hardest to fulfil. But when I spotted an advert in the paper recently for a 'roller conga' record attempt in Glasgow, it felt like it was meant to be: this one just fell into my lap. It was to be held at the Riverside Museum, and the plan was to break the record for the longest unbroken chain of roller skaters, for at least 10 minutes.

'Sounds easy enough,' I remember thinking. How wrong I was!

I rallied the troops for this one, thinking it would be fun to do it with as many people as possible. A combination of friends, cousins and other relatives all signed up to help me.

It'd been years since I've been on a pair of roller skates. Do you remember when we got pink Barbie ones for our birthday one year, and used to skate up and down the hall in them, clinging to one another to stay up? Gary got a black and gold pair, didn't he, and was a real daredevil out on the street, jumping on and off the kerb, but you and I couldn't do much more than skate in a straight line holding hands.

I hoped I'd be a bit better on skates now than I was then, but figured that with so many other people doing it too, they could hold me up if necessary! And if all else failed, I knew it would give you a laugh that my record-breaking attempt involved something we'd both been so rubbish at.

Anyway, we all agreed to stay in the night before, wanting to be fresh and full of beans for our attempt the following morning – but you know how easily led I am, and when some of my colleagues suggested a quick drink after work, I couldn't say no. Anyway, one drink became two, and then a third, and I woke up the next morning feeling absolutely rubbish.

There were 15 of us doing it, in total, and we'd all arranged to meet at Katrina's for breakfast and to travel to the museum together.

'You look terrible!' Katrina said, when she opened the door to me.

'I swear I only had three drinks. I shouldn't feel *this* bad. It's not fair,' I grumbled, as I tucked into a bacon roll to try and cure my hangover.

Once we reached the museum, though, and we saw the metal barriers that had been set up to create a rink, despite my banging headache I felt really excited about being a part of something so fun. There were lots of people all milling around, putting on the skates that were being handed out to all the wannabe record breakers, while a man with a megaphone shouted directions. We quickly put on our skates and all got into the conga line to skate slowly around the rink, never breaking the line.

It was so much harder than it sounds, Nicole! There were 254 of us in total and people kept falling over, or breaking off from the line, so then we would have to start again and again. Meanwhile I was becoming tired and grumpy – you know I've never been good with a hangover! Even Martin, who's super competitive and a bit of a perfectionist, crashed into the barrier at one point. When we all laughed at him he claimed he had 'no choice' as he didn't want to skate into a wee girl. I think he was fibbing to save his pride, though.

Eventually we managed to skate in an unbroken line for 17 minutes and the official from the Guinness World Records declared we'd set a new world record! We were all given a certificate and then we trooped off to the nearest pub for a celebratory drink.

I stuck to Diet Coke.

We agreed that while you definitely wouldn't have been impressed at our skating skills, you'd have been pleased we'd all come together to do this for you. Family and friends were your whole world, Nicole, weren't they? Your wish has helped them all a bit today. I saw how happy they were heading off home, their certificates tucked under their arms, beaming at what they'd achieved.

Even though you're gone, you're still giving us all so much happiness, sis. Me especially. And speaking of happiness, I definitely didn't expect the next of your wishes to be as much of a laugh as it turned out to be ...!

'Milk A Cow'

Unless it's cute little dogs like LouLou and Ralph, me and animals don't really mix, especially big, smelly farmyard ones like cows. You were much more of a Doctor Dolittle, weren't you? I remember you insisting on patting all the donkeys on the beach the year we went to Blackpool on holiday. And do you remember the time you were in Gartnavel and I was allowed to take you out in your wheelchair for some fresh air? You told me you wanted to feed the ducks that lived on the pond next to the hospital and I dutifully obliged. You never mentioned a family of swans lived on the pond too – probably because you knew I was absolutely terrified of them! I stood nervously while you chucked bread to them, which you'd saved from your breakfast, but as they swam nearer and nearer to the bank, then started to waddle towards us, I freaked out.

'We need to go, Nicole,' I pleaded anxiously. 'Swans can be really aggressive – they can break people's arms, you know!'

I started pushing your wheelchair as fast as I could, the swans following us.

'Take me back to the duckieeeeeeees!' you shouted, laughing your head off at my terror.

'No chance!' I shouted back, puffing and panting as I pushed you back up the hill to the hospital. When we reached the entrance I stopped, gasping for breath, while you sat in your chair roaring with laughter.

'Oh, Melissa,' you said, 'you're such a wimp! They're just birds, they weren't going to harm us. They just wanted the bread!'

I started laughing too, thinking how ridiculous we must have looked – me pushing you at top speed with a pack of swans behind us, while you demanded to be taken back to 'the duckieeeees'!

So, a born-and-bred city girl, I had absolutely no idea where I was going to find a cow to milk. They're not exactly just wandering around the centre of Glasgow, are they? In fact, it was Alana who made your 'milk a cow' wish happen, after she discovered there was a dairy farm in Barrhead, just outside Glasgow. She contacted the farmer, explained about your list and he invited us to come and milk one of his cows.

Obviously I was grateful she'd gone to all the trouble of arranging it all, but the thought of getting up close to a smelly cow and, even worse, having to milk it, turned my stomach.

On the day we were to do it, I met Alana wearing my oldest clothes – there was no chance I was getting poo or milk on any of my best outfits! Katrina decided to come along for this one, too. I think she thought it would be fun watching me do this.

We drove to the farm and as soon as we got out of the car, the smell hit me like a ton of bricks. It was vile, Nicole! I was nearly sick! The farmer led us into a massive barn where there must have been over a hundred cows all waiting to be milked.

I had imagined I'd be milking the cow by hand, into a bucket, like in the olden days, but clearly I'm such a city girl I'd no idea that things have moved on quite a bit since then and nowadays it's all done by machine (I'm sure you knew that, though). And so when the farmer told me that all I needed to do was place a big set of suction teats on a cow, and a machine would do the rest, I nearly passed out with relief.

It was still pretty grim, though. The cow smelled and kept stamping her feet menacingly as I tried to get the teats on her massive udders – she obviously knew I was a total novice! And Katrina and Alana stood behind me giggling as I tried not to breathe in the smell of the barn or leapt with fear every time the cow mooed or moved.

It took about five minutes but eventually I got the teats on and we watched the milk flowing from the cow into a massive tank.

'I've done it!' I cried. 'I've milked a cow!'

'Er, Melissa … there's something on your face …' Alana said, stifling a laugh.

I grabbed my compact out of my handbag and stared at my reflection. There was a big streak of brown right across my forehead where I had wiped away the sweat from the effort of trying to get the teats on the cow!

'Oh, my God,' I said, horrified, scrubbing at it with the sleeve of my coat. 'That had better be mud and not poo!'

We laughed all the way home, the windows of the car rolled right down because we all stank of the farmyard.

You probably thought, because you were such an animal lover, that it would be easy to milk a cow, but I'd like to have seen you have a go, Nicole. Take it from me, it's hard work – I'll never take my glass of milk in the morning for granted again!

Love you so much, little Miss Dolittle. Hope you're proud of me.

La La xxx

Letter Three
November 2013

Dear 'Cole,

You had such a silly sense of humour it came as no surprise to me that your list contained quite a few pretty quirky wishes! And I've been hard at work over the last few months making them come true, because these small, light-hearted wishes of yours are every bit as important to me as the bigger, more emotional ones.

Keeping busy helps me keep my grief at bay. I don't know if it's healthy or not, but I prefer to focus on your list and what I'm going to do next in your memory, than stop and really acknowledge what life is like now you're gone.

All of us are coping in different ways: Dad's thrown himself into his work, Gary just bottles up how he's feeling like he's always done, and Mum spends a lot of time talking about you, reminiscing about all the things you liked, said and did. I know she's terrified her memories of you are going to fade, and believes that if she keeps talking about you that will keep them fresh in her mind. It can be hard, though. Because if I join in, and remember something about you that she doesn't, she gets upset even though I reassure her everyone remembers different things. She likes to tidy your room, too, rearranging your clothes in their drawers and dusting. It's her way of still caring for you.

Last month it was our birthday, Nicole. My first without you.

In the weeks leading up to it, I was dreading it. Just the thought of waking up and not being able to swap presents with you, knowing I'd be going to your grave instead of going out for a girly lunch with you … it tore me up inside. I'd be blowing out the candles on a cake myself and, basically, nothing would be the way it had been for our 21 years together.

You were crazy about birthdays, weren't you? For weeks before you'd talk incessantly about what you were buying me and drop hints about what you wanted me to buy you. From when we were little girls you took on the role of the party planner, deciding who we'd invite, what food we'd have and the games we'd play. I've wondered since if there was a part of you that worried you wouldn't have as many birthdays as other people, and so you wanted to make the most of every single one.

I woke up on our birthday with a sick feeling in my stomach. I didn't want this day – I wanted it to be over because it was just another horrible reminder you're not here. When I went downstairs, Mum and Dad had been up early and decorated the kitchen with balloons and banners, and there was a cake on the table, with 22 pink candles in it.

I knew they were doing their best to stay upbeat and make a fuss of me, but I could see in their eyes they were struggling. I can't even begin to imagine what it's like thinking back to the day your daughter was born, a baby with her whole life ahead of her. And then, what should be the happiest day of every year, celebrating that anniversary, is an unescapable reminder that she's gone, and you have outlived your child.

After breakfast, we went to your grave and took with us 22 yellow balloons, one for every year of your life, just like we'd done at your funeral. Mum and I carried them, while Dad carried a heart-shaped wreath made from yellow flowers.

Mum and Dad like to go to your grave. It's where they feel closest to you, Nicole. But I don't like the thought of you down in the ground – I'd rather go to your room when I want to talk to you, or sit in the garden at night and look up to the stars. I prefer to think you're all around me than just in one place, but it helps Mum and Dad to be able to visit you at the place we said goodbye for the last time.

At your grave, we stood quietly. It was a sunny day, just like your funeral had been, but much colder, and I shivered as the wind whipped around us.

'Shall we release the balloons?' I asked Mum, blinking back my tears.

She nodded and, together, we let go of the huge bunch of yellow ribbons attached to each balloon. But, because it was so windy, instead of floating serenely up into the sky as we'd planned, they blew in every direction around the graveyard, bouncing off headstones and getting stuck in the hedges! In an instant our tears turned to hysterical laughter as we chased them, trying to catch them, before anyone saw.

'Well, that will have given Nicole a good laugh on her birthday,' Mum said, out of breath from charging around the graveyard.

Once we'd finally got the balloons up into the sky – splashes of colour against the steely grey October clouds – we walked slowly back to the car, me in the middle with Mum and Dad's arms wrapped around me.

'I hope she saw us running around like headless chickens.' I laughed. 'She'd have loved that.'

It's not been an easy few weeks getting through this milestone, Nicole, and I don't know what I'd have done if it wasn't for your wacky wishes to lift my spirits.

'Fart In A Lift'

Definitely one of your most ridiculous (and embarrassing) wishes! Why on earth would you want to do that, Nicole? I have no idea, and can only blame it on your incorrigibly naughty sense of humour.

I chickened out of doing it several times – in the lift at a shopping centre and then in a car park – because both times the lift was packed with people and I just lost my nerve. Then, one day, I was on a training course for work. After a very spicy Mexican wrap for my lunch I was feeling a bit … shall we say, *gassy*. Standing in the glass lift of the posh building where we'd come to for the day, surrounded by strangers, I just impulsively decided to do it. I didn't know anyone in it, and I wouldn't have to see them again if they realised what I'd done, so it seemed like as good an opportunity as any.

And so … I let one rip. There was a parping noise and then an unmistakable whiff, and I could see a few people around me wrinkling their noses in disgust. I was blushing like mad but kept looking innocently ahead, praying we'd reach my floor before anyone realised I was the culprit. I couldn't get out of the lift fast enough, half ashamed of myself, and half delighted I'd managed to do it.

Martin couldn't believe I'd done it when I told him that evening, because as you know I'm usually so shy about bodily functions.

'Does this mean you'll be farting in front of me now?' he joked.

'Definitely not!' I replied. 'This was a one-off for Nicole, and *never* to be repeated.'

'Go Skinny-dipping'

Talking of embarrassing wishes … thanks to you, Nicole, I can now call myself a flasher. Yep, that's right, me – who won't even go topless on holiday!

You wanted to go skinny-dipping, but while I imagine you pictured yourself doing it on holiday somewhere hot and sunny in a lovely warm sea, I had to do it in Scotland in the middle of winter.

A few people have asked me why you wanted to do this and I think I know why. If you'd had a lung transplant, you'd have been left with a big scar across your chest, but you wouldn't have been ashamed of it. To you, it would have been a symbol of your survival against the odds, and you'd have been proud to show it off. And what better way to do that than go skinny-dipping?

Martin and I decided to turn this wish into a night away and checked into a country hotel in Troon, on the west coast of Scotland. After a romantic dinner and a night in our lovely room, I woke up the next morning. Just for a second I'd forgotten why we were there – and then I remembered …

After breakfast – of which I ate practically nothing because I was feeling sick at the thought of stripping off in public – Martin drove me to the beach nearby. Thankfully it was deserted, apart from a woman walking her dog at the other end. I hoped she was a slow walker so she wouldn't get a fright at seeing me in the buff! The reason the beach was so deserted, however—? The lashing rain and howling wind.

'Of all the days I could have picked to do this …' I moaned, staring out of the car window.

'No backing out now!' Martin laughed. 'And before you ask, I'm definitely not joining in with this wish. You're on your own for this one!'

Reluctantly I wriggled out of my jeans, top and underwear until I was sitting totally starkers beside Martin.

'Ready?' he asked, grinning mischievously. 'I've got a blanket on the back seat for when you've done it, and I'll put the heating on full blast.'

'I bet Nicole is laughing her head off at me right now,' I said, as I opened the car door, immediately shivering as the freezing air hit my naked skin.

Stepping out of the car, I looked at the water, which was around 20 metres away. 'Ready, steady, go!' I screamed and ran down the beach as fast as I could, praying no one would spot me.

I kept running, right into the water, and the bitter cold took my breath away as if I had been physically winded. I dived under the waves, and then immediately turned around, wading out of the water and began running back to the car, wrenching open the door and flinging myself back into the warmth as Martin laughed loudly at me.

I think the whole thing was over in less than a minute but it felt like for ever, and I have never been so cold in all my life, Nicole! I was actually blue when I got back into the car.

Martin wrapped the blanket around me as I shivered uncontrollably. 'Well done, Melissa – you did it! Now we just have to hope your toes don't drop off from hypothermia,' he said.

Later that day, once I had defrosted, I thought about how, because of your cystic fibrosis, Mum had had no choice but to wrap you up in cotton wool, especially when we were younger.

A chest infection, or even just a cold, could have been fatal for you and so you were kept indoors a lot. Playing out in the cold or rain was never allowed, as Mum couldn't risk you getting ill because your body just couldn't handle it the way mine could.

The surprise of that cold, the exhilaration of the moment – that was for you, sis.

'Dance In The Rain'

I'm sure your protected childhood was responsible for your next wish: to dance in the rain. It might seem like such a simple thing to other people, but to you that would have been a massive milestone after a transplant, wouldn't it? To have been 'normal' enough to go out and get cold and wet, without worrying that a sniffle could see you end up in hospital.

Last month, I was at an open-air DJ gig in Glasgow with our friends Joanne and Lisa, and Alana. Of course – typical Scottish weather – it was pouring, and I'd had to abandon my cool clubbing clothes for a pair of wellies and one of Mum's raincoats.

Standing in the rain, I was starting to wish I'd stayed in and not bothered coming when the song 'Wake Me Up' by Avicii began to play. I absolutely love it and immediately started dancing like crazy in the mud, lost in my own wee world.

It was Alana who grabbed my arm and shouted above the booming music: 'You're dancing in the rain! You're doing one of her wishes!'

I stopped dead, raindrops running down my face, people dancing all around me. I hadn't even been thinking about this wish, but she was right – I'd just done it. And with that realisation I burst into tears. I think I just wished so much you'd been there, dancing like a maniac and not caring about being soaked to the bone with me.

The girls all hugged me and reassured me they understood why I was upset, then suggested we all troop off to the bar to dry off and have a drink in your memory. We toasted you with bottles of your favourite Archers Aqua Peach alcopop, as our sodden clothes dried in the warmth of the bar, and you won't be surprised to hear that I woke up the next morning with a cold from my soaking.

So thanks very much for that!

'Get Arrested'

As if getting naked and getting soaked weren't enough, I've also got myself arrested for you, Nicole.

Goody-two-shoes me wasn't sure about doing this one, but you loved crime dramas and police shows and I know you'd have found it hilarious to even pretend to have been in trouble with the law.

I had no idea how I was going to make this one happen, short of actually committing a crime, and I wasn't prepared to do that – even for you, sis! I just wanted a slap on the wrist, not an actual criminal record which I'd have for ever.

Facebook came to my rescue after I posted a message asking for help with this one. Within minutes, our cousin Kevin got in touch to say he had two police officer friends and was sure he could arrange a fake arrest for me. He explained he wasn't sure when they'd be able to do it, as it would depend on how busy they were dealing with real criminals, but he'd be in touch.

I didn't hear anything from him for a few weeks, and I wondered if he'd forgotten or maybe his friends had refused. Then, last weekend, I was at home lounging in my pyjamas, watching a football match on TV with Mum, Dad and Martin, when my phone beeped with a text message: *The police are on their way.*

'Oh my goodness!' I squealed. 'I'm going to be arrested and I'm in my pyjamas!'

And, as if on cue, at that moment a big police van pulled up right outside our house and two officers, a man and a woman, got out of it, looking incredibly stern.

'What will the neighbours think?' Mum said, laughing. 'They'll wonder what on earth is going on.'

The doorbell went and Dad answered it.

I couldn't stop giggling nervously as they came into the living room.

'We're here to arrest you, Melissa Tennant,' the male officer said, smiling broadly. 'We'd like to help you make your sister's wish come true.'

Standing up, I had to put my hands behind my back so they could put a set of handcuffs on me. Martin and Dad sat on the sofa roaring with laugher at the sight of my wee, spindly wrists in the heavy cuffs – they were almost too big for me!

'You're under arrest, Melissa,' the female officer said, and I could see she was trying not to laugh. 'Come with us.'

They frogmarched me out of the house and into their van, past a crowd of neighbours who'd gathered in the street to have a nosy at what on earth was happening. After a quick drive around the block, they dropped me back home, where Mum, Dad and Martin were standing waiting on the doorstep for me as Mum tried desperately to explain to the neighbours that it was all a set-up and I hadn't turned to a life of crime!

'Learn To Juggle'

I've been on a real roll with your wishes, Nicole, and somehow I've found the time to learn to juggle, using a set of balls I bought online and watching 'How to juggle' videos on YouTube. As you were always the entertainer of the family, I can just imagine how much you'd have loved to know how to juggle, and shown off your skills to everyone.

Remember when we were very small, I think no older than four, and Mum and Dad took us to the circus in Glasgow? Some of the other children there were absolutely terrified of the clowns but we were fascinated by them and spent ages afterwards trying to teach ourselves to juggle (unsuccessfully) until every apple and orange in the fruit bowl was bruised.

So, this time round, I wasn't hugely confident I'd be able to master juggling for you, and at first I was a complete liability – balls were flying everywhere, and one of Mum's best vases got broken, which she wasn't too happy about. But, after practising every night, I can now juggle with three balls. So that's my new party trick!

Mind you, it's not quite so easy after a few drinks, I can tell you …!

'Learn Archery' and 'Fire A Gun'

I can also now add archery and shooting to my repertoire of newfound talents thanks to you, after spending a day with our cousin John at a shooting ground in Ayrshire.

He was one of the people who was with you when you passed away, and even though he's, what, 17 years older than us? I feel very close to him for that reason. When I didn't have the strength to stay with you that awful night, he did, and I'm so grateful to him for that. And so I wanted to involve him in your wishes.

Together we spent an afternoon, along with Martin, learning how to shoot huge shotguns and playing with bows and arrows. I surprised myself by not being too bad at either. With the guns we did clay pigeon shooting and the boys couldn't believe it when I hit the clay time and time again; it was the same with archery, with me hitting the target the most.

The boys were raging that I beat them – I'm sure it was just beginner's luck, though!

You had a fiery temper, Nicole, and I think you'd have loved both. I found it a great way to let off steam and I came away buzzing from it. What a great idea, 'Cole – typically you.

'Go To A Football Game'

On top of all these crazy wishes, I got to spend a lovely afternoon with Dad, just the two of us, thanks to your list. With him away working so much and me busy with work and getting through your list, it's not often we get much father–daughter time.

You'd wished to go to a football game, so Dad and I got tickets recently for a game at Ibrox Park, between Rangers and Stenhousemuir.

Technically, you'd been to a game, in fact, when we were 13. I'm sure you remember when you entered a local newspaper competition to be a flag bearer in a guard of honour at a testimonial match for the Celtic player, Henrik Larsson, and won. I remember as if it were yesterday. You'd been off sick that day, after telling Mum you didn't feel well enough to go to school. Yet at 4 p.m., when the phone rang and it was the newspaper saying you'd won and had to be at Celtic Park in an hour, you leapt off the sofa, got changed out of your pyjamas and ran out of the door, dragging Mum with you to drive you to the football ground!

'Talk about Lazarus!' Dad joked at the time. 'So much for being too sick for school. It's a miracle!'

We watched the game on TV that evening and were so excited when we caught a glimpse of you lining up with all the players before kick-off. 'There she is!' I'd squealed. 'There's my sister!'

I felt so proud of you standing out on that pitch in front of thousands of people, Nicole, a massive grin on your face. You didn't often get to do really exciting things like that, and I was so happy you'd had this chance.

You got home late that night buzzing with excitement about all the famous players you'd met, saying that next time you wanted to be in the stands to actually see a game as a fan.

Well, I've done that for you. The match Dad and I went to was on Armed Forces Day so the ground was filled with soldiers, their families and people who had lost a loved one. To know that I was surrounded by other people who've been through the pain we have, of losing someone they love – it felt like it was fate we'd picked that game to watch.

A woman beside me was standing, wiping away tears, so I offered her a tissue. She explained her son had died in Afghanistan, but had loved football, so she'd come in his memory and was wearing his Rangers shirt. I told her all about you, and how we were here in your place, too. We looked at each other and something passed between us – an unspoken under-standing of what the other was feeling and, before I knew it, we were hugging one another, surrounded by cheering football fans.

It was a strange moment. As you know, I'm not in the habit of going round hugging strangers. But meeting someone else, outside our family, who knew just how I feel ... I felt such a solidarity with her.

Rangers won the game so Dad and I were happy, but what was even better was having the time alone with him. Since you've gone, Nicole, my relationship with Dad has definitely changed. You and I were always Daddy's girls, but I'm even closer to him now. He and I are very similar and we both have a habit of bottling things up, but now we're more open about how we feel. I think we've all realised that life is so short, that you have to be honest with the people around you. Walking home from the football we talked about how we both missed you so much.

'It's like there's a piece of my heart missing,' Dad told me. 'You don't expect to bury your children, and a part of me went with her into the ground. It's hard to explain ...'

I took his hand, like I used to do as a little girl, and squeezed it. 'I know just what you mean, Dad,' I said quietly. 'I've felt incomplete since she died, and I think I'll always feel this way. It's just something we have to learn to live with. It's why I'm trying to fill that emptiness with her wishes, knowing I'm doing something to make her happy. You've helped me do that today.'

What I'd thought would just be a fun day out at the football actually ended up being quite an emotional one, Nicole, but in a really good way. Without you, we've had to galvanise as a family, and it's the strength of our love for you which is the bond which helps us through every day.

'Get A Piercing'

Oh my goodness, I almost forgot to tell you – I got my ears pierced!

You already had yours done, so when I saw this on the list I knew you'd been planning to have a more unusual piercing, like in your tongue or belly button. But I thought I would stick to something simpler!

We both got our ears pierced when we were one, didn't we? But then, when I was about seven, I took mine out to do sport at school one day and by the time I remembered to put them back in, the holes had closed over. For years I've been meaning to get them re-pierced but kept putting it off as I was scared it would be sore, so having to do it for you was a good excuse to 'man up', as you used to say, and get on with it.

A couple of Saturdays ago, I was at our local salon having a manicure with Katrina and Alana, when Alana spotted a poster advertising ear piercing.

'Why don't you get your ears done now?' she suggested.

My stomach did a backflip. I'm such a wimp with pain that I had planned to do it alone, not in front of people. But then all the ladies in the salon got really excited about being part of your list, and I didn't want to disappoint them, so before I knew it I was agreeing to have it done.

'At least I'll be able to throw out all my Pat Butcher-style clip-on earrings!' I joked, as the lady prepared the piercing gun with a pair of tiny gold studs.

I sat in the chair while Katrina held my hand (she knows what a baby I am) and Alana took photos on her mobile phone, giggling at how pale I'd suddenly gone. In the end, it was over so quickly, and really didn't hurt, that I felt a bit daft for having been so nervous. Now I can't wait for six weeks to pass, so I can change the starter studs and treat myself to some lovely dangly pairs!

I hope you're impressed at how busy I've been recently, sis. I feel so happy to complete each wish, knowing it's what you want. Just like when you were alive, I'd do anything for you, no matter how silly, embarrassing or painful it may be.

All my love,

La La xxx

Letter Four
January 2014

Dear 'Cole,

It's 2 a.m. and I'm so tired I can hardly keep my eyes open. But I couldn't wait to write to you and tell you all about today.

Since we were little girls, we've both been utterly fascinated by the stars, planets and space, haven't we? Do you remember the year we got a children's telescope from Santa? Some of the other kids in the street would tease us for being geeky but we didn't care – we loved anything astrological.

If it wasn't cold or wet at night, Mum would sometimes allow us to wrap up in warm blankets and sit in the garden, gazing up at the sky through our telescope and trying to count all the stars and name the constellations.

We'd lie side by side on the grass, holding hands and talking in hushed whispers about what might be out there.

'We're just a tiny little piece of the universe, Melissa,' you would tell me, in a very serious voice. 'For all we know, there could be other twins called Nicole and Melissa out there living on another planet. I hope, if there is, that Nicole doesn't have cystic fibrosis.'

'See The Northern Lights'

Before I even finished reading your list of wishes, I knew this one would be on it. It was in 2007, when the movie *The Golden Compass* came out, that we both learned about the Northern Lights. You spent hours on the computer reading about them and looking at photos and images of this amazing natural light display.

'It's incredible,' you'd mutter, completely entranced as we watched *The Golden Compass* for the hundredth time, just for the scenes which showed them. 'I would *love* to see it with my own eyes one day.'

'We'll go together, Nicole, just you and me, when you're better,' I'd say, silently hoping that day would come, haunted by the pessimistic voice in my head which said it wouldn't.

Well, today, Nicole, I went to see the Northern Lights for you. And it was every bit as amazing as you'd hoped it would be. I can only begin to imagine how completely blown away by it you would have been – I'd have given anything for you to have been there, to have seen your face. If you'd felt anything like I did today, it would have shown the most intense mix of amazement, awe and sheer joy. It was like nothing we'd ever experienced before.

At first I wasn't sure how I was going to do this wish because it was one of the most expensive ones on the list. Trust you, Nicole – you always had expensive tastes! I didn't want to let you down but I didn't know how I was going to afford it. So when Laura phoned from her work in the travel agency to say a holiday company had offered me two free flights to go and see the Lights, because they wanted to help with our list, I was ecstatic.

It couldn't have come at a better time, either – after our first Christmas without you, I really needed something to cheer me up. I had been dreading it. Christmas has always been such a big thing in our family, especially for you, who'd be shopping, wrapping and hiding gifts for weeks beforehand. Your excitement was infectious, and without it I just had no idea how we were going to get through the day.

All of us knew it wasn't going to be the same without you, but we felt we had to try. We knew you wouldn't have wanted to see us all moping around at Christmas, and we felt that we owed it to you to try and just make the best of it, as hard as that was going to be.

In the morning, as well as going to see Gran's grave, we went to yours too and brought you two floral wreaths in the shape of Westie dogs. Then Dad, as ever, cooked lunch (he managed not to burn anything this time – a Christmas miracle!). John came for lunch and it helped not having that empty seat around the table, then we all went to Auntie Anne's in the evening so we could be with other people, to distract us.

For me, the hardest part of the day was seeing Mum leave a bundle of wrapped presents on your bed in the morning.

'She's still my wee girl, and she'll always get a Christmas gift from me,' she said, wiping away a tear. 'I don't want her to be forgotten about.'

All she wants is to keep you with her in every way she can, Nicole, and if buying you presents helps her, I think it's a great idea. Something we've all learned since you died is that there's no right or wrong way to grieve – it's different for every person.

Knowing I had this special wish ahead was what helped me through Christmas, but I knew I had to pick someone to come with me, and I knew instantly who I wanted to help me fulfil this one: Gary.

I've been trying to involve as many of our family and friends in the wish list as possible, Nicole. You were loved by so many people, and they all want to help in any way they can to make your dreams come true. I wanted to do one of the most special wishes with Gary – not something that was silly or funny, but one that we both knew would mean so much to you. This one felt like the obvious choice. And I couldn't believe how touched he was when I asked him a few weeks ago to come with me today.

I phoned him one evening after work – he's not living at home any more, as he's moved in with his girlfriend, Ayisha.

'Hi, Gary,' I said. 'I've got something really important to ask you. I need your help with one of Nicole's wishes. Will you come and see the Northern Lights with me in a few weeks' time?'

'Are you sure?' he said. 'I mean, I'd really love to do this with you, Melissa, but I know there must be loads of other people lining up to help.'

'Yes, but Nicole only had one baby brother, and that's you. And I think she'd love us to go and do this together.'

There was silence at the other end of the phone and I knew Gary was fighting back tears. 'Thanks, Melissa,' he replied eventually. 'I'd love to.'

You know what Gary's like, Nicole – he rarely lets anyone see how he's really feeling. He's always been like that. When you were sick, and even at the end, when you were dying, he'd hide away in his room rather than come to the hospital. He just couldn't cope with seeing his big sister ill, so he avoided having to deal with it. In fact, it drove me crazy at times. Everyone else had to face the fact you were seriously ill, and just get on with it for your sake. I used to think sometimes that Gary was selfish, putting himself first, but I realised over time he just wasn't able to watch you slip away.

He loved you so much, he couldn't bear to see you suffer.

Since you died, Gary and I haven't spent a lot of time together, just the two of us – when I see him, there's always other people there, like Mum and Dad, or Martin. I thought this trip would be a good chance for us to just hang out, brother and sister.

For 20 years we were both one of three, and now there's just us two. We need to get used to that, as painful as it is.

This afternoon I picked up Gary and we drove to Glasgow Airport to catch our flight. We were both really giddy in the car, excited about what lay ahead.

At the airport, we were directed into a private room, with around a hundred other passengers, for a pre-flight presentation from a pair of astronomers. They told us all about what causes the Northern Lights, and what constellations we should look out for.

I was getting more and more excited, thinking how much you'd love this crash-course in astronomy, but when they explained that there were no guarantees we'd be able to see the Lights, my excitement turned to anxiety. What if I wasn't able to see them and fulfil your wish? I knew I wouldn't get the chance to take this trip again for free. My stomach was in knots worrying about letting you down, praying I wouldn't.

We boarded the plane and took off, heading north in the direction of the Shetland Islands. On board, the two astronomers who'd hosted the seminar were there to answer any questions people had.

'Can you imagine Nicole?' Gary laughed. 'She'd have had them tortured with questions!'

He was right – you were always so inquisitive, Nicole, wanting to know everything about anything. From teachers at school to the nurses and consultants who treated you in hospital, you were infamous for your never-ending list of questions.

As you know, I'm not the world's best flyer so when the air hostess announced some time into the flight that the lights in the cabin would be going off so we could see the Northern Lights properly, I panicked. I grabbed Gary's arm, my heart pounding as we sat in pitch darkness, flying high above the earth.

'Calm down,' he said, putting his arm around me to give me a squeeze. 'You're such a scaredy cat. Nicole will be having a right giggle at you.'

Slowly I relaxed a bit and took some deep breaths, focusing instead on what we were hopefully going to see in just a few moments. And, suddenly, the captain's voice made an announcement: 'If you look out of the left-hand windows of the plane, you can see the Northern Lights now.'

My heart began to pound with anticipation as the plane circled to the left, and suddenly, there they were. Nothing could have prepared me for the sight of the Northern Lights, and my skin instantly broke out in goosebumps.

The night sky was filled with a shimmering curtain of glowing colours: green, magenta, blue … a haze of the most incredible, softly glowing shades. It was magical, eerie and beautiful all at the same time. I quite literally couldn't breathe for a few seconds, I was so stunned by the beauty in front of me. It's probably one of the very few times in my life I've been completely speechless.

Gary and I held hands and I began to cry. Some tears were happy ones – that I had been given the opportunity to see something so incredibly beautiful; but mixed with them were tears of frustration and sadness that you weren't getting to see it too, Nicole.

And then, just then, the strangest sensation washed over me. It was like a feeling of warmth, as if I was being hugged by an invisible presence, and instead of feeling sad I only felt a deep happiness.

Was that you, Nicole? Were you there with me, somehow?

The plane circled for over an hour, allowing us plenty of time to soak up the beauty of it all. And I could imagine your face in my mind, Nicole, all that time, with a look of complete awe and happiness on it.

I feel like we had a glimpse into another world, there was something so magical and other-earthly about it. We were brought up Catholic, weren't we, and taught there was a heaven and an afterlife. Growing up, though, I was never as sure as you that this was true. A part of me always wondered was death the end, and was there nothing after that? You refused to accept that, though, adamant that the people we knew who'd passed away, like our grandparents and your friend Gaynor, had gone on to a better place.

Did you have a sense death would come to you sooner than the rest of us, so you had a greater reason to believe it wouldn't be the end?

Since you died, I've thought a lot about an afterlife and now, like you, I believe in one. I can't accept that your spirit and your soul – what made you who you were – could just be extinguished. Seeing the Lights strengthened the belief that you're out there somewhere, watching over me from a beautiful place.

I feel like I've had a glimpse into a life beyond our earth. The Northern Lights were like a gateway to another place – they're the closest I think you can come to Heaven while you're alive.

After an hour, the plane turned around and we headed back to Glasgow Airport. The cabin was quiet, all of us lost in our thoughts and wonderment about what we'd just been lucky enough to see.

Of all your wishes, today's is the one that will stay with me for ever: I'll never forget it. Thanks to you, Nicole, and your wish list, I've just had one of the most amazing experiences of my life. But it was bittersweet, because I *so* wished we could have done it together.

Wherever you are, I hope it's as beautiful and peaceful as the Northern Lights, and there are no hospitals, or feeding machines and painful injections. You're fit and strong, and never held back by disease. That's what I hope Heaven is like for you.

Love you,

La La xxx

Letter Five
January 2014

Dear 'Cole,

I can hardly write this letter I'm giggling so much thinking about the day I've just spent. Never in a million years did I imagine I'd spend a Saturday afternoon lying as naked as the day we were born on a table in front of a room full of strangers!

My reputation for being a bit of a prude is well known, isn't it? I'm pretty sure the only people who've seen me with my top off since we hit puberty are you and Martin. The communal changing rooms at school after PE or the local leisure centre were my worst nightmare, and you'd laugh at me trying to get dressed and undressed behind a towel, like a contortionist.

Thanks to you and your wish list, I'm finding myself in situations I never would normally, but do you know what? I'm loving it! I was always happy to be the twin in the background, the quieter one, and let you take the lead. But your list has pushed me out front, and although it's sometimes scary, or embarrassing, or often both, it's good for me.

'Pose For A Life Art Class'

You can imagine my initial reaction when I read this wish on your list. My stomach tied itself up in knots at the very thought of stripping off and posing for strangers, even if it was in the name of art.

And, maybe not surprisingly, this has been one of the only wishes no one has volunteered to do with me: 'Absolutely no chance. I'll do anything else but that one,' seems to have been the most common response when I've asked friends and family if any of them wanted to join me in getting their kit off in your memory!

I can't say I blame them!

So I knew I was going to be on my own for this one, and in a way I was glad. 'Maybe,' I thought, 'it will be easier doing it in front of strangers than with someone I know.' Or so I hoped at least!

'You'll never go through with it,' was Mum's reaction when I told her what I was planning to do next. 'You'll get to the door and then run a mile, I bet!'

I did some research online about life drawing classes in Glasgow, and came across one held every week in a room at the Botanic Gardens. The organiser, a man called Sandy, was so nice when I spoke to him on the phone and explained that my crazy twin had wanted to be a life art model, and I was doing it for you. We met for a coffee last week and he explained that to be a model for the class, I would have to pose for two hours, with some breaks, doing a variety of poses. The class, he told me, was a mix of students – people who do it as a hobby, and professional artists.

'And will I have anything on at all?' I asked him nervously, desperately hoping he would say I could have a sheet draped over me.

'Nothing, I'm afraid,' he replied, and chuckled when he saw my anxious face. 'But don't be nervous. It really is a very relaxed and private atmosphere. The students are only interested in you as something to draw – they really don't care who you are or what you look like.'

'Easy for you to say,' I thought. He wasn't the one who was going to be stripping off!

I went away still feeling incredibly nervous and embarrassed about the whole thing. The thought of people getting to see my wee, tiny boobs made me shudder. What if the class didn't think I had a good enough body to draw?

Anyway, Sandy texted me yesterday saying a model was needed for a class being held today and if I was still interested, did I want to come along? Every part of me wanted to back out and tell him I just couldn't go through with it but before I knew it I found my fingers typing a reply: *Brilliant, I'll see you tomorrow.*

'What am I letting myself in for?' I moaned to Martin last night, over dinner.

231

'Why do you think Nicole put this on her list?' he asked.

'You know Nicole,' I replied. 'She loved not following the crowd – anything that was scary or unappealing to other people, she wanted to do it.' Then I thought a bit more. 'And you know the scene in *Titanic*, when Leonardo DiCaprio draws Kate Winslet nude, the night the ship sinks? She loved that scene and used to rewind it to watch it over and over again.' I smiled. 'She found it so romantic, and she really admired Kate Winslet's confidence in showing off her body. I think she thought that once she was free of cystic fibrosis, after a transplant, she'd feel more confident about her own body, and doing something like this would have been such a great way to show off that confidence.'

I know you were self-conscious about your body, sis, and I understood why. It told the story, clearer than words ever could, about what you had endured during 21 years of illness. You had a scar on your stomach from your feeding tube, puncture marks from the hundreds of needles you'd been stuck with, and the steroids you had to take made you puffy and swollen. You were tiny, just five feet tall, but you seemed even smaller because you were so stooped over. And while most girls our age were constantly dieting to lose a few pounds, one of your biggest challenges was trying to gain weight as the cystic fibrosis stopped your body absorbing the nutrients and calories it needed.

You used to say to me that once you had a transplant, and your body had had time to heal and recover from everything it had been through, you wanted to show it off. Knowing all of that, this wish of yours makes perfect sense to me. And I wouldn't have done it for anyone else but you.

I woke up this morning and for a few seconds I forgot what lay ahead. Then I remembered, and buried my face in my pillow, already blushing with embarrassment at the thought of what I was going to do!

Even though they weren't prepared to join in and be models too, Mum, Katrina and Martin had all offered to come with me to keep me company. But I wanted to go alone! I thought it would be easier to zone out and forget what I was doing if only strangers were looking at me, instead of people I knew. I was also really worried one of them would make funny faces at me and I'd get a fit of the giggles, which wouldn't have been very professional, would it?

I fake-tanned last night, which Martin thought was hilarious.

'You're still going to be naked, so why are you bothering doing that?' he laughed, as I slathered it on.

'I always feel better when I've got a tan, so I'm hoping it'll help me feel a bit more confident instead of flashing my pasty white winter skin!' I replied.

Before I left this morning, I took one of Dad's old shirts from his wardrobe and stuffed it in my bag so I'd have something to wear during the breaks, then set off for the Botanic Gardens.

I was too early and had to wait for around 15 minutes before Sandy arrived to set the room up for the class. By the time he arrived I'd worked myself up into such a tizz I was on the verge of pulling out. 'What the hell am I doing here? I can't go through with this,' I kept thinking. 'I'm going to text Sandy and say I'm sick, or my car's broken down, or I've had to go to work today …' But just as I was trying to come up with an excuse he appeared.

'I'm so glad you've come!' he exclaimed, genuinely thrilled to see me. 'I'm sure your sister would be really happy you're doing this for her.'

I could hear your voice in my head, Nicole, encouraging me: 'Come on, Melissa. Do this for me. Don't be shy!'

Reluctantly I shuffled into the room behind Sandy, only my determination not to let you down making me put one foot in front of the other. He showed me a little changing room where I could take off my clothes and put Dad's shirt on, and I got undressed, shaking from a combination of nerves and the room being a bit chilly.

'I can't believe I'm doing this for you, Nicole,' I whispered out loud. 'I bet you're having a really good giggle at me!'

As I slipped Dad's shirt on, I could hear the class starting to arrive, footsteps filing past the door of the changing room and men's and women's voices mingling.

'It's fine, Melissa,' I reassured myself. 'In two hours this will all be over, you'll have ticked another wish off the list and you'll never see any of the people here today again.'

I stepped out of the changing room, clutching Dad's shirt tightly to me to preserve my modesty for a few moments longer, and stopped dead when I saw a woman with shocking ginger hair walking into the room. So much for my hope I'd be posing for total strangers – she was an art teacher from our old school! Even though she'd never taught me, and probably hadn't a clue who I was, I still blushed beetroot red.

'Are you ready to start?' said Sandy, leading me into the centre of the room.

The class of around 15 people were all standing at their easels, waiting for me. In front of them was a long table, covered in a white cloth, which was where I would sit, lie and pose for the next two hours.

For a second I stood, completely frozen, then before I completely lost my nerve I shrugged off the shirt and climbed up onto the table.

I felt sure my heart was going to explode out of my chest it was beating so hard, but when I saw that none of the artists had even batted an eyelid and were too busy getting their pencils and paintbrushes ready, I relaxed a little. Sandy had been right – I was just an object to them, no different to a vase of flowers or a pretty landscape. They didn't care if my boobs weren't big enough or I had a bit of cellulite on my thighs. And it made me realise, with a lurching feeling of sadness, that this was something you could have done while you were alive, Nicole. You wouldn't have needed to wait until you'd had a transplant and you felt your body was 'better' and more attractive. In fact, your body – with all its scars and evidence of your illness – would have been so interesting to draw.

I'd thought someone would tell me how to pose for the class, but it was up to me to decide. At first I was unsure what to do and just sat with my legs crossed, with one hand across my chest and the other on my knee. But as I relaxed into it I lay down on my side, stretched out, with my head resting on my hand, so my body was completely exposed.

And it was then that I got a fit of the giggles, because it was just like the scene you loved from *Titanic*! As I giggled, the class looked at me very seriously so I bit my lip and did my best to look very thoughtful and elegant.

After two hours with just two short breaks, I'd done 15 short poses and two long ones, before Sandy announced that the class was over.

Climbing down from the table, putting my shirt back on, I felt stiff and sore from staying still for so long, but also elated. I'd done it, Nicole! And not just that – once I'd got over my initial nerves and embarrassment, I'd really enjoyed it.

The whole day's been a learning curve for me, sis, about my own body confidence and not letting my self-consciousness hold me back. It's been another gift from you through your list.

If only you'd had the confidence to do something like this before it was too late. The way you were before you died, and how you felt about your body, I understand why, for you, it was something to do in the future when CF was behind you. But I think if you'd plucked up the courage, like I did today, to say to hell with what I look like, you'd have absolutely loved it. You were so beautiful, Nicole – any artist would have been lucky to draw you. I just wish you had been able to see your beauty yourself, like I could.

Anyway, I hope you're proud of me and finding it as funny as I am that in 15 houses in Glasgow tonight, there's a drawing of me in the buff!

Love you so much,

La La xxx

Letter Six
February 2014

Dear 'Cole,

Or should I say, 'Bonjour, Mademoiselle Nicole!'?

Well, if that's not a giveaway to the latest of your wishes I've been fulfilling, I really don't know what is! I'm writing this letter from Charles De Gaulle Airport, where we are waiting for our early morning flight home.

I've been in Paris for the weekend, sis, making another of your dreams come true. And it was every bit as Ooh la la as I know you imagined it would be.

For as long as I can remember you were fascinated by Paris. You loved films set there, and I remember you poring over travel guides about the city as your bedtime reading. Its reputation for being so stylish and sophisticated, not to mention romantic, captivated you, and you'd daydream about strolling along the Seine, arm in arm with some French hunk. Don't deny it!

As you know, I'm much more of a beach holiday sort of girl. I'd rather laze in the sun and do very little than go to a big city. But you loved the episodes of Sex And The City when Carrie

Bradshaw moved to Paris, and you'd talk incessantly about how you wanted to watch a cabaret show at the Moulin Rouge and see the *Mona Lisa* at the Louvre.

Out of the two of us you were definitely the culture vulture, Nicole. You'd tease me about just wanting sun, sand and cocktails when I booked a holiday, while I'd rib you about wanting to 'soak up the atmosphere' of a place and visit boring art galleries.

It was just one of our differences I loved so much. That we could be such polar opposites in some ways, but still be bonded tighter than glue, for me summed up what was great about being a twin.

'Climb The Steps Of The Eiffel Tower'

When I found your list last summer, I knew a trip to Paris would be on it, but I wasn't expecting the wish to be so specific about climbing the Eiffel Tower. In the past, we'd looked into taking you to Paris, even for just a few days, but it was just impossible: so reliant on your oxygen tank as your lungs got worse and worse, and being so weak and fragile, getting on a plane just wasn't an option for you. The thought of you taking a bad turn, thousands of miles from home and the doctors who'd treated you all your life, was just not something any of us were prepared to risk, you included.

And even if we had been able to get you to Paris, you would never have been able to climb the Eiffel Tower. When I think back to how you were, especially towards the end, it's simply inconceivable. You could barely get up the stairs at home without help because you were so breathless and in pain, let alone climb 704 steps.

Knowing you planned to do this wish after a lung transplant is so poignant. And it makes it hurt doubly as much to know what a difference it would have made had you got one. What better way would there have been to show the world how fit and well a new pair of lungs had made you, than by taking on a physical challenge like this? It would have been the ultimate 'up yours' to cystic fibrosis, wouldn't it? The proof it was in your past, and that you weren't fragile, breathless Nicole, who had to be pushed to the shops in a wheelchair any longer.

It just makes me so *angry* when I think about all those things you wanted to do, Nicole, but cystic fibrosis held you back. It was like a dark, dark cloud hanging over you all your life. Why did it have to be you with this horrible disease?

I'm sorry, I don't want this letter to be filled with anger – I know you hated it when I got wound up about the unfairness of your illness.

I'll tell you about your Parisian wish instead.

This was, without doubt, one of the most emotional ones so far, Nicole. At times it hurt my heart because I so wanted you to be there, but I tried to stay upbeat and soak up all the sophistication, beauty and buzz of the city you were so eager to see.

I looked at Paris through your eyes, Nicole, and I grew to love it.

I have to admit I wasn't very excited about doing the wish in the first place. Call me uncultured if you like, but tramping around a big city in freezing February, not to mention climbing hundreds of steps … not really me, is it, sis? A big part of me wished you'd wanted to go to an exotic beach resort instead! But I could hear your voice in my head telling me not to be so boring and lazy and, as your wish is my command, I dutifully booked flights for Mum and me.

And, now that I've been, I'm more than happy to eat my words about not looking forward to this wish – just like I've eaten delicious croissants non-stop for the last 48 hours! In fact, I dread to think about the Parisian pounds I've put on. How do French women stay so slim and elegant? It's a mystery to me when they're surrounded by so much delicious food!

Mum and I flew from Glasgow Airport last Thursday evening, arriving late in Paris. Exhausted, we went directly to our hotel, and straight to bed. As shattered as I was, though, I couldn't sleep. My mind was racing, thinking about the challenge we would be taking on in the morning. I knew it was going to be physically tough – let's face it, neither Mum nor I are what you'd call super fit! But I also knew how emotional it was going to be. To have come all this way, to do something so important to you – I knew it wouldn't be anything but heartbreaking. But I didn't want it to be all sadness; I wanted to look back on this weekend and feel happy too, because we'd made such a beautiful wish of yours come true.

Careful not to wake Mum, I climbed out of bed and crept to the hotel room window. As far as the eye could see were the twinkling lights of this gorgeous city and, in the distance, the Eiffel Tower stood, lit up against the night sky.

It was like a beacon, watching over its city. It was so huge, too … was I really going to be able to climb every step of it in the morning?

'I'm here, Nicole,' I whispered in the darkness of the bedroom. 'We're here for you. Wish me luck for tomorrow. I know you'll be with us every step of the way.'

The next morning, we breakfasted at a perfect little café near our hotel, down a cobbled side street. You'd have just loved it, sis – it was so typically Parisian! I could imagine you sitting at the little corner table, scribbling out an itinerary of everything you wanted to see and do.

Mum got such a fit of the giggles when I ordered our breakfast of coffee and croissants in my very poor schoolgirl French, which set me off too. The waiter looked on bemused as we both rocked with laughter, tears streaming down our faces. He must have thought we were crazy!

I'd chosen Mum to do this wish with because I wanted some time alone with her, just to be together, to talk if she wanted to, and to help give her some closure by knowing she'd been able to make one of your dreams come true. She was so thrilled when

I told her I'd booked flights for us. Seeing her smile again and look forward to this trip, I knew it had been the right decision to bring her.

After breakfast – and more giggles at my attempts to ask for the bill – Mum and I set off on foot for the Eiffel Tower. As we walked, I began to realise why this city had so fascinated you. It was so *bustling* – everywhere I looked there was something interesting to see, from rows of street artists with their easels sketching and painting on the pavement, to patisseries with their windows piled high with pastel-coloured *macarons*, the smell of brioche wafting out from within. Beautifully dressed women, so sophisticated and elegant, walked past us, and Mum and I giggled at how much we stuck out like sore thumbs in our cosy Primark puffa coats and flat shoes, both prioritising warmth and comfort over style!

If you'd come to Paris, you'd have planned your wardrobe for months in advance, Nicole, wouldn't you? Determined to fit in with the locals and be as chic as possible.

When we reached the bottom of the Eiffel Tower it was bedlam. There were coaches dropping off hordes of tourists from all over the world and people queueing to get on the lifts that go up and down the tower all day.

'Are you ready?' I asked Mum.

'Let's do it,' she said, smiling. 'Let's do it for Nicole.'

I'm probably stating the obvious here but the climb was *exhausting*. Up and up we went, our breath making tiny clouds in the freezing air. It didn't seem to matter how far we'd climbed, there were always just more and more steps to go.

'Come on, Mum,' I encouraged her, when she stopped for a breather around halfway up. 'Not far to go now.'

'Well, that's a fib if ever I heard one!' But she laughed, taking my arm as we began to climb again.

Finally we reached the second floor, 115 metres off the ground, which is as far as you can go via the stairs. Stepping out onto the viewing platform, surrounded by safety netting, tourists speaking languages from all around the world milled around us. Mum and I stood in their midst, arms around one another as we caught our breath and took in the breathtaking view in front of us.

There was Paris, stretching out as far as the eye could see. I could see Notre Dame, the setting for one of your favourite Disney films, and the lush Luxembourg Gardens right in the centre of the city.

'She'd have just loved it, wouldn't she?' said Mum quietly. 'I wish she could have seen this with her own eyes.' And then, out of her handbag, Mum produced a small padlock. 'I read about people leaving padlocks on the bridges in Paris, as a symbol of love, but now we're here I think we should leave it here instead,' she said.

'I think that's a great idea, Mum. And I've got something I'd like to leave, too. It's one of the memorial cards we had made for after her funeral,' I replied.

I took the small card out of my wallet and looked at it. On it is a beautiful photo of you, Nicole, taken at our eighteenth birthday party. At the top are the words: 'Always Remembered'.

Together we clipped the padlock to the wire meshing and tucked the card securely into it.

And Mum completely broke down.

I held her in my arms – the way she used to hold us when we were little girls – as she sobbed. 'I miss her so much, Melissa,' she wept. 'Why did I have to bury my baby? Why was she taken away from us? All we have are these wishes, but it's just so hard knowing she should have been doing them herself.'

I couldn't speak, battling to hold back my own tears because I so wanted to be strong for her. Hugging Mum tightly I could sense the agony radiating from her. What can it be like to lose the child you carried inside you, gave birth to and raised? I hope I never find out.

Once Mum had stopped crying we stood together, looking out at Paris.

'We did it,' I said. 'We did it together. I think she'd be proud.'

'I'm proud of you, Melissa,' Mum said, turning to me and gently stroking my cheek, her eyes puffy from crying. 'I don't know where you are finding the strength to fulfil all these wishes. You are an amazing sister to Nicole.'

After our epic climb we decided to be lazy and take the lift back down. 'Well, she never said we had to climb down as well as up!' I joked. At the bottom of the Eiffel Tower, we were both suddenly ravenous. 'Come on, let's go for a fancy lunch in Nicole's honour,' I said. 'My treat.'

We found a lovely restaurant nearby, with tables covered in white linen tablecloths and sparkling crystal glasses. It was so posh, Nicole, you'd have been in your element, nosying at all the well-dressed people tucking into their lunch!

Thankfully our waiter spoke English, which was a relief, as I wasn't sure if my schooldays French was going to stretch to ordering lunch.

'I'll have the croque monsieur,' I said, my tummy rumbling at the thought of the hot toasted sandwich filled with gooey Gruyère cheese.

'Can I have the snails, please?' asked Mum.

I nearly fell off my chair! That's right, Nicole – Mum, not exactly known for being an adventurous eater, ordered snails! If I hadn't been there I wouldn't have believed it, either.

'You're having snails?' I asked incredulously.

'When in Paris …' she replied, sipping the glass of champagne we'd both ordered to celebrate our achievement. 'Nicole would be very impressed, I think.'

'She definitely would,' I said, clinking my glass against hers.

After lunch we spent the afternoon strolling around Paris, popping in and out of shops and galleries. I wanted to soak it all in for you, Nicole, this city with which you felt such an affinity.

Lying in bed last night in our hotel, I felt shattered but satisfied. Everything had gone so perfectly, and now I was another wish closer to making all your dreams come true.

'*Bonne nuit*,' I whispered in the darkness, remembering some more of my almost forgotten French. '*Je t'aime*, Nicole.'

One day I will come back and climb the Eiffel Tower again. And there, at the very top, tucked into the wire, will be that photo of you, Nicole. Always remembered, just like it says on the memorial card.

You never made it to Paris, but a piece of you will always be there now.

Love you so much,

La La xxx

Letter Seven
May 2014

Dear 'Cole,

This letter is coming to you all the way from sunny Lanzarote!

Martin and I are here for a week's holiday and I thought I'd update you on everything I've been up to recently while sunning myself ... I believe that's called multi-tasking!

Don't worry, I'm not slacking – I've actually ticked off one of your wishes since we've been there. I picked Lanzarote for our holiday because, after doing lots of research, I knew it would be a good place to carry out the next wish on your list. And while it's probably not most people's priority when choosing a destination, let's face it, it was going to be pretty hard for me to do in Scotland, wasn't it? Short of breaking into a zoo, I knew this wish was going to have to be done abroad, and it has given us a good excuse for a holiday.

It's the first time Martin and I have been away together as a couple by ourselves, and it's the first time I've been abroad since my holiday to Spain last year, just before you died.

I've found it impossible not to think back to that trip, and before we left for Lanzarote I felt so nervous. I kept thinking, 'Look what happened the last time … what if I go far away again and something terrible happens again?'

Dad's away working in the Shetland Islands at the moment and Gary's living with his girlfriend, so I was going to be leaving Mum at home on her own. But when I confessed to her that I was feeling anxious, she told me I was just being silly, gave me a huge hug and told me to go and enjoy myself. My skin immediately prickled with goosebumps, though, because it reminded me so much of the night before I left for Spain, when you'd done exactly the same thing.

But, just like you had refused to entertain any suggestion of me not going away last year, I knew Mum wouldn't hear of it either, so I tried to put my anxiety out of my mind and just look forward to spending time alone with Martin.

Sitting on the plane to come here, it didn't feel like 10 months since that horrendous journey from Spain to Glasgow, knowing you were slipping away, terrified I was going to be too late to say goodbye to you. Everything, from the roar of the plane's engines as we took off to the sound of the drinks trolley being pushed down the aisle, transported me back to those awful hours as I raced home to you. It'd felt like that journey would never end, and yet I knew when it did I was going to have to face the most awful experience of my life.

The pain I carry deep inside is still very raw, Nicole. I feel like a different person now. I was a girl then but I think grief, and learning to live without you while supporting Mum, Dad and Gary, has made me grow up a lot, into a woman.

But I need to stop looking back – this is meant to be a happy letter! So, back to our holiday …

'Ride A Camel'

While other people have been a bit bewildered about why this wish is on your list, I'm not. I remember how, when we were younger, Dad used to joke that he was going to take us all on holiday and swap Mum for a camel if she didn't stop nagging him! You and I thought this was hilarious and used to dissolve into fits of giggles at the thought of a camel coming to live in our house with us. You'd say that when it came, you'd ride it up and down our street, and wave to all the neighbours like you were some sort of Arabian princess. You were such an animal lover too, that even a smelly camel wouldn't have bothered you.

I booked Martin and me a camel riding trip for the third day of our holiday. We spent the first two days by the pool relaxing. It's been really nice to spend time together, just the two of us. Since you died, we've seemed to spend a lot of time with family and friends, as if we've subconsciously stuck together for strength and support. So it's nice to have an excuse to just be alone together.

The morning of the ride we were collected by coach at 8.30 a.m., along with lots of other holidaymakers who had the same plan as us. Martin couldn't have looked less enthusiastic if he'd tried! He'd much rather have stayed by the pool, but he wanted to play his part in helping me complete your list.

We were driven to a national park and as soon as we stepped off the coach the smell hit me. Oh, Nicole, it was vile! A huge group of camels were waiting for us, lying on the sand, and they stank like nothing I've ever smelled before! Pinching my nose to keep the stench out, I gingerly made my way towards them, avoiding the steaming piles of camel poo that were everywhere. That was when I heard Martin swearing profusely behind me.

'What's wrong?' I asked, turning around.

'I've stepped in poo! In my brand new trainers!' he wailed.

Sure enough, the bottom of one of his dazzling white trainers – which he'd bought especially for the holiday – was covered in fresh, smelly camel dung.

I couldn't stop laughing and was completely unable to help him clean his shoe, which he was doing on a patch of scrubby grass nearby. I don't think he was very impressed at my lack of sympathy!

Shoe drama over, we followed the tour guide to our camels. Each had a saddle across its back with a seat on either side so two people could ride it at once. I climbed into my seat first but when Martin got into his, because he's so much heavier than I am, we were totally unbalanced – my seat was too high and his was too low. The men looking after the camels had to put sand-bags in beside me to balance us out.

The sun was beating down as we set off on our trek. It was very bumpy and we had to grip the sides of our seats so as not to fall out. I felt a bit motion-sick but that was nothing compared to Martin, who was sheet white and absolutely terrified every time the camel let out a loud bellow. Then, just when I thought it couldn't get any more uncomfortable, our camel began to spit … before doing a huge fart!

I seriously thought Martin was going to jump out of his seat and run back to the coach at that point!

The ride only lasted around 15 minutes but it felt MUCH longer, and I was very relieved when we could get off and head back to the pool to recover from our stinky adventure with a stiff drink.

Now, though, I keep laughing, thinking about you riding one of those smelly beasts up and down our street in Glasgow. Nicole, I know you had visions of being like an exotic princess but, trust me, there's nothing remotely glamorous about riding a camel!

'Record A Song In A Studio'

Before I came away on holiday, I spent an afternoon with some of the girls you were closest to, making another of your wishes come true.

Remember when we were younger, you would pretend to be Tina Turner and blast out 'Proud Mary', pretending your hairbrush was a microphone? You always made me be Ike because his part is easy and he was just in the background – which was just as well, as I don't have a note in my head!

I bet recording a song in a studio was one of the things you were most looking forward to doing. While I'm completely tone-deaf, you were a lovely singer, when you weren't too breathless from your cystic fibrosis. Do you remember when we were 14, you took part in the school talent show and sang the song 'Beautiful' by Christina Aguilera? You loved the song because of its message – that it didn't matter what you looked like or what was wrong with you, because beauty comes from within. It was like your anthem for a while, and you played it incessantly on your CD player. I was off sick that day and missed it, so when you came home beaming with pride because you'd come first, I was gutted that I hadn't got to see you perform.

And you'd sing all around the house, all the time, wouldn't you? Anything, from pop songs to hymns. One day I came home from work to find you and Mum singing, 'Hi Ho Hi Ho It's Off To Work We Go' from *Snow White And The Seven Dwarfs* while marching around the living room. At first I thought you'd both gone mad but then I thought, 'What the hell!' and joined in.

The house is so quiet now without you singing away like a little canary. It's one of the things we all say we miss the most about you. So this wish had you written all over it, and I knew it was one to get your best girlfriends involved with.

It felt good knowing we were going to be remembering you in a really fun way and I bounced out of bed the morning we'd booked the studio, eager to get started on this wish. I'd invited Katrina, Gemma, Lisa, Joanne and Chelsea to take part in this one and we met in the car park of the studio, all of us giggling nervously and cracking jokes about how terrible we were going to be.

In the studio, we were given a list of around 20 songs to choose from. Most of them were quite cheesy, like 'Reach For The Stars' by S Club 7 and 'Build Me Up, Buttercup' by The Foundations but, as I scanned the list, one jumped out at me, and the hairs on the back of my neck stood up.

'Oh my goodness, look,' I said, showing the list to the girls. 'We can sing "Let Her Go" by Passenger, from Nicole's burial.' It felt like a sign from you, Nicole – your way of telling me yet again that you were with me, watching over me as I fulfil your wishes. 'I know it might be hard for some of you to sing it, as it's going to bring back some painful memories, but I think it's what Nicole would have wanted us to do. It feels like it's meant to be, doesn't it?'

All the girls nodded, as stunned as I was that this song was on the list.

'And this will be a good way to give us some happy memories when we hear this song from now on, instead of just sad ones,' said Katrina.

As we filed into the recording room and were each given headphones and a microphone on a stand, I was thinking about how much you'd have loved it, Nicole. You'd have felt like a real-life rock star, and been in your element.

As the words to 'Let Her Go' flashed up on a large screen in front of us I joked to the girls that it was a bit like karaoke but without the cocktails! Then, suddenly, the opening chords of the song filled our ears through the headphones.

Instantly, I was transported back to your graveside, watching those yellow balloons float high in the sky as shovelfuls of earth were heaped on your coffin. I remembered the birdsong competing with the sound of crying from around the grave, and how much I struggled to accept, as your coffin disappeared from view, that I'd never see you again.

I still can't really get my head around that.

Next to me, in the studio, Katrina began to cry at the sound of the music, and it was like a domino effect as, one by one, all the girls broke down.

I waved through the glass for the studio technician to stop the music, and took off my headphones. 'Come on, girls, Nicole wouldn't want us all standing here crying. She'd want us to belt out this song for her and enjoy ourselves, just like she would have done. Shall we try again?' I asked.

Wiping away our tears, we all gave themselves a bit of a shake, took some deep breaths and then we were ready to start again.

It took a couple of takes because every now and then one of us would giggle at how terrible we were as a group, or we'd miss out a line by accident, but eventually we'd recorded the whole song.

'You need to think of a band name to have printed on your CD,' the studio technician said. 'What do you want to be called?'

We hadn't realised we'd need a name so had nothing prepared, and I was wracking my brains for inspiration when Gemma piped up from the back of the group: 'What about Nicole's Angels?' she suggested.

'Ooh, I love that,' I said. 'It's perfect!'

Before we were given our CD to take away with us, our song was played over the studio's speakers. We were falling about laughing, Nicole! Some of the girls weren't bad but my tuneless voice and Katrina's broad Glaswegian accent were hysterical. She sounded like one of The Proclaimers! Something tells me record labels won't be beating a path to our door to sign up Nicole's Angels any time soon.

In the car park we all kissed and hugged goodbye, copies of our CD in our handbags. I drove home feeling high a kite. Another wish done but with so much laughter and fun too, and I know that's just how it would have been if you'd been there too, Nicole. Although you'd have been absolutely mortified at my dreadful singing and probably (and quite rightly) switched my microphone off! The CD is hidden in my bedside drawer, and it's for my ears only.

I have 'Let Her Go' on my iPod and I listened to it this morning as I lay by the pool, here in Lanzarote. It still reminded me of your funeral but now I have happy memories too, of laughing and joking with the friends who love you so much. And that feels good.

Got to go and work on my tan, sis, so will sign off for now.

Love you lots like Jelly Tots,

La La xxx

Letter Eight
June 2014

Dear 'Cole,

'Imagine walking down the street and people recognising you because they'd watched you on TV,' you used to say excitedly. 'How cool would that be? And I'd want to be known for having a talent, not just being famous for the sake of it. Like being an amazing singer or actress.'

You always used to tell us that one day you'd be famous, and we'd see you on TV. I could never understand why the thought of being beamed into people's houses across the country held such appeal, but it completely thrilled you.

You were always so determined to make your mark on the world, and maybe being on TV was a really public way to do that. Your cystic fibrosis made your world such a very small one, usually limited to home, hospital, and the immediate area where we lived, that perhaps the thought of millions of people knowing who you were, and watching you, would have given you the sense of achievement that you were more than just a sick girl from Glasgow?

'Be On TV'

While your wish to be on TV after you'd had a transplant made perfect sense, that didn't stop it filling me with dread! I like to think I've come a long way since you've died, Nicole – pushing myself to the front of life through your wishes, instead of being happy in the background. But the thought of having a camera stuck in my face, knowing I was being broadcast into the living rooms of perfect strangers, made me feel sick with nerves.

I could just imagine you chuckling away at my horror and, not for the first time, I wished my twin could have been just a tiny bit shyer in her ambitions! But a promise is a promise, and I knew there was no way I was going to duck out of doing this for you.

For months after discovering your list, I'd no idea how I was going to pull off this wish. How on earth was I going to get myself on TV? I kept pushing it to the bottom of the list, hoping for some inspiration about how to make this one happen. Then, in February 2014, out of the blue I got a private Facebook message from a woman called Jayne, who worked for a small production company called Mac TV. Based in the Shetland Islands, they make a lot of programmes about people in Scotland. They had heard about your death, Nicole, and wanted to interview me as part of a programme about twins, to be shown on the BBC later in the year.

They wanted me to talk about you, our relationship as twins and, of course, your death and how I was coping with losing you.

My gut reaction was to say absolutely no way: being in a TV programme would be bad enough, but to have to talk about life without you felt far too raw. I wasn't ready emotionally to do something like that, and I was worried I'd end up making a complete fool of myself. But, at the back of my mind was the niggling thought that maybe it was meant to be: that maybe this wish could about us as sisters. Wouldn't this be more meaningful than doing something silly like applying to go on a TV quiz show, or jumping in front of the camera during an outside news broadcast – both of which I'd considered doing as a way to fulfil this wish? To speak about you, and tell so many people about how amazing you were and how much I missed you, seemed much more worthwhile.

Part of me wondered if you'd somehow made this happen. Had you brought this opportunity to me because you wanted a very public tribute to our twin bond? You were always so proud to be a twin, so was this your way of sharing that pride with the world?

After several sleepless nights, tossing and turning while I decided what to do, I eventually rang Jayne at the production company.

'OK, I'll do it,' I said. 'I'm really, *really* nervous but I don't want to miss this opportunity to fulfil another of my sister's wishes.'

A couple of days later, I met one of the show's producers, a man called Alastair, at a café in Glasgow. Seeing how enthusiastic he was about the programme, and how moved he was hearing about you and your death, helped settle my nerves a little about the whole thing. I trusted him to treat the story of our life together, and your death, sensitively. After all, I had to think about all our family and friends who'd watch it too, and be mindful it might not be easy for them to see me remembering you.

Alastair explained that they'd really like to interview Mum and Dad for the programme too, and I promised to ask them if they'd take part with me. But you can probably guess, Nicole – they point-blank refused when I asked them that evening over dinner.

They're such private people and I completely understood that for them, their grief at losing you is not for public show. But we had a laugh wondering where on earth you got your extrovert streak, Nicole, when the rest of us are so averse to the limelight! And they gave me their blessing to take part in the programme, even suggesting I ask Katrina to do it with me instead. She was always more like a big sister to us than a cousin, wasn't she? I knew she had the closeness to you that the producers wanted, and so many memories to share. So I phoned her that evening and she agreed immediately.

'I can't say I'm massively keen about going on TV but I want to help you as much as I can with the list,' she said. 'So count me in.'

I agreed with Alastair that Katrina and I would be free the following week to do the filming at her house. Putting down the phone after making the arrangements, I felt so ridiculously nervous. Remember when we were little girls, Nicole, and you loved being filmed with the family camcorder, singing, dancing and just chatting away? You'd watch the tapes back, over and over again, delighting in seeing yourself on screen. I always avoided the camera like the plague, cringing at the sound of my voice or how I looked if I accidentally popped up in one of your films. Whenever possible, I'd volunteer to hold the camera, always feeling more comfortable behind it than in front of it.

Now though, there was no going back, and I was going to have to get over my camera shyness very quickly!

The night before the filming was St Valentine's Day, and Martin took me out for dinner and to stay at a lovely hotel. It was so sweet of him, but it was wasted on me because all I could think about was the next day. Knowing I was going to be speaking publicly about you, Nicole … it felt like your funeral when I delivered the eulogy, all over again. I wanted to do it properly and not completely break down, but I just didn't know if I was going to manage it.

I lay awake in our luxury hotel room worrying, Martin snoring beside me. Then I laughed, thinking how you'd be rolling your eyes at me 'getting my knickers in a twist' as you used to say, at just talking on camera for a few moments. You'd have said I was a scaredy cat and told me not to be so silly and just enjoy the experience, wouldn't you? Oh, how I wished I had your bravery!

The next morning, Dad phoned me on my mobile. 'I've changed my mind,' he said. 'I'd like to help you with this wish if that's still OK. I'll meet you at Katrina's.'

Part of me couldn't believe Dad had agreed to take part. A quiet man, I knew coming to this decision wouldn't have come easily to him but I was so happy he'd be by my side.

An hour later I arrived at Katrina's.

'I'm so nervous,' I said, as we did our hair and make-up in her bedroom mirror. 'Look, my hands are shaking!'

'What we have to remember is how much Nicole would have loved the chance to do this,' Katrina replied. 'She'd have been beside herself with excitement at the thought a camera crew were on their way, just to film her.'

'You're right,' I nodded. 'She'd have been in her element.'

Dad arrived, a bundle of nerves, closely followed by the production team laden down with cameras, microphones and sound booms.

'Let's do this,' Katrina said. 'Let's tell everyone how wonderful our Nicole was.'

It didn't take long before Katrina's living room resembled a TV studio, with a large camera on a tripod, and three seats in front of it for me, her and Dad. A bright light that the crew had set up shone down on us and we each had a small microphone clipped to our clothes.

Dad looked as nervous as I felt and I had to keep wiping my palms on my jeans because they were so horribly sweaty. Finally, after a lot of soundchecks and adjusting of the camera, we were ready to begin.

'Try not to look directly into the camera,' the interviewer said. 'Look at me instead.'

I've no doubt it would have come easy to you, Nicole, but my stomach was in knots. It felt so strange to be sitting in Katrina's living room with a camera right in my face, and a stranger about to ask me personal questions which I knew were going to be very hard to answer.

At first, my answers to her questions were short. I knew all my emotions were bubbling close to the surface, and I was afraid to talk too much in case I became upset. The interviewer asked about our childhood, and what it was like for me when you were ill.

It was when she asked me about whether I believed that twins have a psychic connection that I couldn't hold back my tears any longer. Memories of how unsettled I was on my holiday in Spain, and how I hadn't wanted to go in the first place, came flooding back. 'I had such a strong feeling something bad was going to happen, and that I shouldn't leave her. I know that was down to a special bond between us. I only wish I'd trusted my instinct …' I sobbed. 'It was the same when we were little girls. If she fell off her bike and hurt her knee, I'd tell Mum mine hurt too. Every part of us was entwined. It's hard to explain, but she really was the other half of me. Our connection went far beyond sisters.'

Dad and Katrina cried too, when they spoke about you.

It was so much more painful than I could ever have imagined, especially hearing Dad talk about holding you for the first time when we were born, then kissing you goodbye when you died. You know he's not a man who shows his emotions easily, but watching him be so honest and open about his love for you, and his deep pain, I felt really proud of him.

The mood lifted when we each had to be filmed walking in and out of the room, and looking through family photo albums. 'It's like we're in one of those really staged reality shows,' Katrina joked. It felt good to laugh after such an emotional afternoon, and good to remember that we were doing this to make you happy, Nicole.

Afterwards we walked to the local pub for a well-earned drink. 'Here's to being TV stars!' Dad said, as we clinked our glasses together. 'Nicole had us wrapped around her little finger when she was here, and nothing's changed since she died. Who'd have thought the three of us would end up on television?'

That afternoon was four months ago, Nicole, and between then and now I'd practically forgotten that the programme still had to air. Then, last week, Jayne called to let me know it was going to be broadcast on BBC Alba that evening.

I was half nervous, half excited to see it. I didn't know what parts of our interview would be shown and what would have been edited out. Not to mention how I'd look and sound on TV.

I decided to watch the programme alone. I knew I'd probably get upset seeing myself talk about you, and if I did, I didn't want to have to explain how I was feeling to anyone else. We were just one part of the programme that other twins had taken part in, and I felt jealous the others still had one another, when I was talking about losing you. And, seeing photos of you flash up on the screen, then me, Dad and Katrina all sharing our memories of you, I just couldn't hold back the tears. It was so emotional, but I also felt a sense of happiness that, in a very roundabout way, you'd got on TV, which was something you'd always wanted.

I definitely don't think I have a future as a TV star, but knowing that people across Scotland now know about you, and how amazing you were, I feel proud and glad I did it.

And that's not all I've been up to for you recently, sis!

'Go To A Wedding'

You were such a romantic, Nicole – a believer in true love, and you were fascinated by weddings. You loved the dresses, the flowers and the venues, never missing an episode of *Don't Tell The Bride* and buying wedding magazines from the corner shop to exclaim over. For you, one of the most exciting things about being a bride would have meant being the centre of attention – for all the right reasons, and not because of your health.

267

But, more than all that, you loved what a wedding day stood for.

'Imagine finding that one person that you want to spend your whole life with, and making a commitment to them in front of everyone important to you. Just the thought of it gives me goosebumps,' you used to say, a wistful smile on your face.

Something I wanted most for you, Nicole, after a lung transplant, of course, was for you to meet that person. You'd have grabbed your chance at lasting love and never let go, but you never got the chance. And the fact that you never even got to go to someone else's wedding just hammered home how unfair it is that you died so young, never getting to see any of our friends or cousins tie the knot.

So when an invitation landed on the doormat a few months ago, inviting Martin and me to the wedding of my friend, Nicola, and her fiancé, Andrew, I was ecstatic. Not only would it be a wonderful day to be a part of, but I'd get to go in your memory.

I wore a coral coloured dress with a black jacket and heels, and Martin wore his kilt.

'Don't you two make a gorgeous pair!' Mum said as we left the house that morning. 'When are we all going to get an invite to your big day, eh?'

'Mum,' I laughed, blushing like mad, 'we're far too young to be getting married! Don't be buying a hat just yet!'

The wedding was at the Brig o' Doon Hotel in Ayrshire, and I tried to soak up every last detail to tell you all about it, Nicole. There were around 120 guests and it was a humanist ceremony, so there were poems and songs instead of anything religious. I thought it was so lovely when the rings were passed around among everyone so we could all be a part of the union they were forming.

Nicola looked incredible in a white satin gown, with a scooped back and very thin straps; the four bridesmaids, which included Katrina, were in mauve. The men were all in matching grey kilts and looked very handsome (although not as handsome as Martin, of course). At the reception, instead of names, each table had a date that was important to the couple – like the date they first met and when they got engaged – which I thought was a really sweet idea.

You'd have just loved it all, Nicole – from the delicious meal to the hilarious speeches and, of course, the dancing afterwards. It was everything I know you thought a wedding should be, full of love and fun. Watching Nicola and Andrew take to the floor for their first dance, I wasn't the only guest there with a tear in my eye. But I knew everyone else's tears were simply those of joy, while mine were also mixed with a deep sadness that you hadn't got to do something as simple as attend a wedding.

I just hope our twin bond is still unbroken, and that somehow you're getting to see, through my eyes, all these wonderful things.

I know you might think, Nicole, that you didn't get to find your forever love. But you did: it's me, and you are mine. Because no romantic love will ever come close to what we had together.

Big kisses,

La La xxx

Letter Nine
July 2014

Dear 'Cole,

It's one year today since you died.

It's so strange even writing those words.

I really can't believe it's been 12 months since you were here, since I heard your voice or hugged you. That awful night when you passed away seems like only yesterday and although life has gone on, the deep pain in my heart hasn't healed. I doubt it ever will, to be honest.

Part of me wanted to hide away today, with the curtains closed and the door locked. To just get through this day, and get it over with, because I knew how hard it was going to be. If I didn't have to see anyone, or speak to anyone, maybe I could pretend it wasn't happening. But I knew that wasn't the right thing to do. I couldn't opt out – I had to mark the date in some way.

Rather than just go to your grave and spend the day quietly remembering you, like people might have expected, I decided to do the complete opposite: 'I'm going to throw a party in Nicole's memory,' I said to Mum a few weeks ago. 'Remember how she wanted her funeral to be a celebration? Well, let's make her anniversary the same.'

'Ride A Mechanical Bull'

Mum thought having a party for you was a brilliant idea, probably recognising that I needed a project to keep my mind busy and that you always loved any excuse to throw a party. 'And, while we're at it, let's hire a mechanical bull and tick off another of Nicole's wishes!' I said. 'No one will have the chance to be sad when they're lining up for a go.'

With help from Katrina, Alana and other friends, I booked the Fairfield Working Men's Club as it's not that far from Mum and Dad's house. We hired a face painter for the kids, a DJ to get everyone up dancing and, most importantly, a mechanical bull!

Goodness only knows why this was on your list, Nicole – it's such a random thing to want to do. But just the thought of you clinging onto a giant fake bull, with your red hair flying over your face, made me giggle when I read it on your list.

After a lot of blowing up of balloons, laying out finger food and decorating, the room we'd hired was ready and this afternoon we filled it with over 100 people, all of whom wanted to spend today with us.

As everyone arrived, lining up to tell me how much they missed you and how proud they were of me for everything I've been doing for you, I could feel myself getting really emotional.

But I'd been determined that this would be a happy day, so I decided to take my turn on the mechanical bull. I knew it would distract me, and give everyone a good laugh!

I think I lasted all of five seconds before it flung me off onto the bouncy mat. You'd have been mortified at how bad I was at it, Nicole, but trust me, it's as hard as it looks! Paul was a bit better, clinging on for 10 seconds, but we all thought you'd have lasted the longest because of your sheer stubbornness.

Watching people get up and dance to all your favourite songs, and share their favourite memories of you with Mum and Dad, I feel sure this has been the right way to spend today and that you'd have approved.

At the end of the afternoon, Rhiannon, Karis and I did some Irish dancing for everyone. It's been ages since I've done it, especially with our cousins. It reminded me of how you would make me good-luck cards before all my competitions and how supportive you always were when it was my hobby.

When the music stopped and our dancing display came to an end, everyone was cheering and I couldn't help but start to cry. I'd been bottling up my emotions all day, focusing on making sure everyone had a good time and that we remembered you in the most fun way possible. But, once I started it was like a floodgate had opened and I had to spend a few moments in the toilet, just calming down a bit.

'Are you OK, love?' Mum asked, coming to find me in the club's bathroom.

'I'm OK now,' I replied, blowing my nose and trying to fix my eye make-up in the mirror. 'She'd have loved today so much, all these people coming just for her …'

'She would,' Mum said. 'And I've no doubt she's been here in some way, laughing at you all getting on that bull and soaking up all the love in the room for her.' Her eyes met mine in the mirror. 'You know how much Nicole loved a good party. She won't have missed this, trust me. Now, come on and enjoy the rest of the party.'

Were you there today, Nicole? I really hope so. Did you laugh at me getting chucked off the bull?

That's another wish of yours fulfilled, and I have a big bruise on my bum to prove it.

'Get Another Tattoo'

You'll never guess what I also did this month for you … I got a tattoo! Yes, *me*, who's absolutely terrified of needles.

I can hardly believe it myself, and was sure I'd back out at the very last minute but, knowing it was what you really wanted propelled me through the door of the tattoo parlour, shaking like a leaf. And it was another way of marking this anniversary, with a wish that I would be permanently reminded of you every time I looked in the mirror.

I'll never forget the day you got your first tattoo, in the summer of 2012. For months and months you'd been telling anyone who'd listen that you were going to get one, but none of us believed you'd actually go through with it. I was absolutely sure you'd chicken out. Not because you were scared of needles – they didn't faze you and you used to joke you were like a pincushion, you'd had so many stuck in you over the years – but because a tattoo is such a permanent thing, and you're stuck with it for ever, I wasn't sure if you'd have the nerve to commit to one.

I was proved wrong when you came home and burst through the front door.

'I did it! I got one!' you squealed. 'Come and take a photo of it so I can show everyone on Facebook.'

You were buzzing, so thrilled with yourself, and I was gobsmacked. There, tattooed in black ink on your right shoulder, were two footprints, each about the size of a thumbnail and the words, 'And Then I Carried You' above them.

I recognised the quote instantly, as it came from one of our favourite poems called 'Footprints In The Sand'. It's all about a dream in which a person is walking along a beach with God, leaving two sets of footprints in the sand. But sometimes there is only one set, usually when the person was having a very difficult time in their life. The person turns to God and asks why, just when they needed Him the most, God abandoned them to walk alone. But God explains to them: 'During your times of trial and suffering, when you see only one set of footprints, it was then that I carried you.'

I gently stroked the tattoo – do you remember? 'It's beautiful, Nicole, really beautiful,' I whispered, in awe of not just your bravery at actually going through with your plan to be tattooed, but that you'd chosen something so lovely.

'It's about me and you,' she replied. 'A reminder to me that no matter what I am going through you, you're always there by my side or carrying me through it.'

I couldn't speak and my eyes filled with tears.

'Come here, you big softie,' you laughed, throwing your arms around me. 'Don't cry – it's my way of saying thank you for everything you do.'

I hugged you back tightly, overwhelmed you'd chosen your tattoo to be a tribute to our relationship.

'And now it's your turn to get one,' you said then, raising your eyebrows in anticipation.

'Me? Oh, Nicole, I couldn't. You know I hate needles! I'd collapse on the floor if anyone even came near me with a tattoo needle,' I said.

'Nonsense, it wasn't that bad, honestly,' you replied. And then you said: 'I'm definitely going to get a second one. I'm keeping any quotes and pictures I like in a little book to inspire me when I go back for another one. Come on, don't be a wimp!'

For months afterwards you would ask me when I was going to get mine, and I kept coming up with excuses like I was too busy at work or I wasn't feeling well. But the truth was I was just terrified of pain and needles. I felt dizzy if I even thought about having blood taken.

Of course, you never got the chance to get another tattoo, so when I saw this wish on your list I knew it was time to put my fears to one side and get one for you.

It took me a long time to decide what design I wanted. It had to remind me of you, as yours did of me, for it to always mean something important to me. And, just like yours, I wanted one that was discreet but still beautiful, so I'd always love it and never regret having it done.

For months, since you died, I've been looking for inspiration … and recently I finally found it.

Remember how we both loved the book *The Death And Life Of Charlie St Cloud*? It's about a boy who survives a car crash which kills his brother, and is all about holding on to people, as well as letting go. We both read it from cover to cover until our copy was dog-eared, with the pages almost falling out from the spine. In it there are quotes from the works of the poet E.E. Cummings, and one line in particular always resonated deeply with us both.

'*You are my sun, my moon and all my stars.*'

It sums up perfectly how I feel about you, Nicole. You were, and are, my whole world, the other half of me, and just because you're gone doesn't mean I don't feel like that any more.

Flicking through the book for inspiration, the moment I read that quote I knew I'd found my tattoo. Yours was a message to me, and this could be my message to you; a permanent reminder of our bond which even death hasn't, and won't, break.

I knew I had to go and get the tattoo quickly, before my fear got the better of me, so last week I phoned a tattoo parlour in Govan and made an appointment for today.

I woke up this morning feeling sick to my stomach with nerves. I honestly can't remember the last time I felt so anxious, not even for exams when we were at school! But I could hear your voice in my head as I got dressed, while Martin and Katrina waited downstairs to take me to the tattoo parlour.

'You can do this, sis,' I heard you say. 'It's not that bad, and it means we can be tattoo twins for ever!'

In the car I was too nervous to speak, and Martin and Katrina couldn't stop giggling at how pale and terrified I looked.

'Why are you making me to do this, Nicole?' I muttered as I got out of the car, my legs trembling. 'Help me get through this …'

Inside the parlour I was shown to a large leather chair which I sat forward on, as I'd decided to have the tattoo on my right shoulder, just like you. Katrina sat beside me on a stool, holding my hand, and Martin stood in the corner.

'Oh, Melissa, I've never seen you look so scared!' he laughed. 'Cheer up, it'll be over soon!'

'Easy for you to say!' I replied, but I couldn't help but laugh at myself.

What a wimp I am compared to you, Nicole! You had years of being jabbed with needles, hooked up to machines and undergoing painful tests, and here I was, making a big drama out of a few moments of pain.

'Would you like some numbing cream put on the skin first?' the tattoo artist asked.

'Yes, please!' I exclaimed. 'Anything you've got that will make it hurt less I'll take!'

Once my skin was numb he got to work, and I kept my eyes tightly closed as I squeezed Katrina's hand.

The buzzing noise of the needle was scary, but thanks to the cream I hardly felt anything. So I couldn't believe it when, after just 10 minutes, he was finished.

'Is that it?' I asked, suddenly feeling a bit foolish I'd been such a drama queen about it all.

'That's it!' he said.

'Nicole was right after all – it really wasn't that bad,' I said to Katrina, smiling with relief that it was over and I'd ticked another wish off the list.

With the help of a mirror and Katrina taking some photos on her phone, I was able to see it. My eyes welled up at the sight of it. 'It's beautiful,' I said. 'It's just perfect. Nicole would've loved it.'

Can you believe I actually went through with it? I know you're probably laughing at me for having the numbing cream, but even so I think I did pretty well for a needle-phobe!

I keep looking at the tattoo in the mirror, getting used to seeing it on my shoulder. I've always been so conservative, probably a bit prim and proper, so it's really strange to see a tattoo on my body. But I really do love it, especially because of the meaning behind it.

It's only been a year since you died, and I have my whole life ahead without you, Nicole. But, even though years are going to pass, and some memories will fade and emotions will get easier, this tattoo will always be a part of me. It's like an imprint of you, like you're here all the time with me, and I love that. I might even add to it in the future, with some little stars around it.

I'm going to show it to everyone I know, and even people I don't, and tell them the story behind it.

You didn't get the chance to have another tattoo, Nicole, but I've done it for you and I hope you're happy that we're finally tattoo twins now.

Love you lots,

La La xxx

Letter Ten
January 2015

Dear 'Cole,

You really do love setting me a challenge, don't you? Of all your wishes, this one has been one of the hardest for me to fulfil, and recently I'd been starting to panic that I wasn't going to pull it off for you. I'm just an ordinary wee girl from Glasgow, after all! So I'm very relieved to tell you that, this month, I infiltrated the world of show business for you, Nicole, meeting some of your favourite stars and telling them all about you! I even did some air kissing like a proper luvvie – next thing you know I'll be calling everyone 'Daaaarllling'!

I will always remember how you were fascinated by celebrities, reading magazines from cover to cover and watching every reality show under the sun. But your favourites were the people who were known for their talent, not just famous for the sake of it – actresses, singers, dancers … they were the ones you were most drawn to. Like them, your dream was to one day be known for something worthwhile.

I think you always felt your cystic fibrosis defined who you were, and that made you determined to carve out a different identity for yourself one day.

And I've no doubt you would have, if you'd had the chance.

'Get My Photo Taken With Three Celebrities'

Last month I wrote to the BBC, telling them about your wishes and how I was struggling to tick this one off. I wasn't really expecting to hear back from them, as I figured they were probably inundated with people wanting to meet their stars, so can you imagine my face when one of the staff from the *Strictly Come Dancing* tour phoned me earlier this month and offered me two tickets to the Glasgow show at the SSE Hydro, where all the big concerts and shows take place, and a chance to meet some of the celebrities taking part?

I was so stunned, not to mention relieved, I only just about managed to stutter out a thank you. Time and time again I've been so blown away by the generosity of strangers in helping me fulfil your wishes – people really are so moved when they hear about you, Nicole. You were special in life, someone that people were just drawn to, and nothing has changed.

You absolutely loved *Strictly*, didn't you? You never missed an episode. You'd watch the TV, transfixed by the sparkling costumes and beautiful dancers, boo loudly if the judges were too harsh with their scores and cheer when anyone scored a 10 for their dance. I knew you were imagining yourself fit and well enough to be twirled around a ballroom floor by a handsome partner, and you loved all the glitz and glamour of the costumes and the sets. So when I got the call about the tour it felt like another one of those little signs from you that have peppered this list: a message just for me that you can see what I'm doing and you're pleased.

Needless to say, everyone was queuing up to help with this wish when they heard I had two tickets ... where were they all when I had to skinny-dip and pose in the nude, eh?

I chose Dianne in the end. Our cousin's a huge fan of the show, and so bubbly and confident – I was worried I might be too shy to walk up and chat to really famous people, but knew she'd have no such problem. She was my insurance policy if I clammed up, because she's not afraid of anything. In that way she's so like you! She's been really keen to help with the list, and I thought this would be a nice one for her to experience too.

We left Mum and Dad's house absolutely buzzing with excitement. Not for the first time I felt both lucky and guilty that your list has opened so many doors for me, Nicole: lucky to have had the chance to do so many things I never would've got to do normally; guilty because it should be you doing them, not me.

Dad drove us to the Hydro. 'Have a brilliant time, ladies!' he shouted through the car window as we tottered towards the entrance in our high heels. 'Tell that Tess Daly I'm a big fan!'

Giggling at Dad, we headed straight to the bar for a few cocktails before collecting our tickets from the box office. Along with the tickets, we were handed a surprise goody bag each containing a programme, a T-shirt and a mug, and then we were shown to our seats, which were amazing, with a perfect view of the huge dancefloor.

Hearing the orchestra warming up, and watching the lighting and sound technicians make their final checks, I had goosebumps, I was so excited. For years you and I envied the *Strictly* audiences, and now I was here to see your favourite programme. It felt a bit surreal and, as always, I wished you were sitting beside me, getting ready to cheer on your favourite couples.

Suddenly the lights went down and the *Strictly* theme tune began blasting out. The dancefloor filled with professional dancers and celebrities jiving, waltzing and doing gravity-defying lifts in their diamante-covered costumes.

The show flew by. We sang along to the songs played by the orchestra, hissed at the judges when they said anything negative and stamped our feet in approval for our favourite couples. At the end, when the lights went up, I'd had such an amazing time I'd forgotten the best bit was still to come – meeting the celebrities!

We made our way to the side of the stage and one of the production team met us there to take us behind the curtain to the backstage area. I felt like such a groupie, Nicole! How many people get to go backstage at a big show like that?

We stood in the middle of the area reserved just for the stars of the show and their friends and family, our mouths wide open in amazement. We could have caught flies! There was Caroline Flack, who'd won the last series, and over there was the gorgeous Thom Evans standing chatting to Alison Hammond and Zoë Ball. I felt like we were on a TV programme ourselves, surrounded by all these famous and familiar faces.

Just at that moment *TOWIE* star Mark Wright came up and introduced himself to us. Oh, Nicole, he's sooo handsome, even better looking than on TV! Somehow I found my voice and explained why we were there and he offered to sign my programme. He scribbled his autograph on it and posed for photos for us both.

'That's one down, two to go!' Dianne said, as we scoured the room for more celebrities.

One of the producers brought Rachel Stevens over to us next, and she was such a sweetheart, happily posing for a photo with us. She's so gorgeous and petite, like a little doll. She reminded me of you in that way, Nicole.

Feeling a bit braver, I walked up to Zoë Ball and explained that I was here carrying out a wish for my sister. She was really moved to hear about everything you'd been through, Nicole, and how we had lost you. When she told Dianne she loved her necklace I thought Dianne was going to explode with excitement. We had a quick photo taken with her, and then it was time to leave.

'Even celebrities love my style!' Dianne said proudly, as we made our way out of the Hydro to get a taxi home.

'You're going to dine out on that for a long time, aren't you?' I teased.

Of every wish on your list, Nicole, I think this one would have been your favourite to do – it was so much *fun*. You wouldn't have been as star-struck as me; in fact, you'd probably have found some way to talk yourself on to the tour bus with all the celebrities after the show. You always had the gift of the gab!

When I got home, the first thing I did was place the programme, signed by all three celebrities, and my ticket for the show, into the memory box I made for you, alongside all my letters to you.

I went to sleep and dreamed of you, Nicole, tripping the light fantastic across a polished ballroom floor, in a beautiful gown with your hair up like a film star.

Wherever you are, I hope you're dancing your heart out.

'Go To Go Ape'

A million miles from the glamour of my night at *Strictly* was my visit to Go Ape the following morning.

With my head a bit fuzzy from the cocktails Dianne and I enjoyed before the show, I dragged myself out of bed at some ungodly hour to drive with Martin to Go Ape in Aberfoyle, in Stirlingshire.

I hadn't had time to do much research into what this wish actually involved – all I knew was that it was some sort of adventure park and I had no idea what lay ahead of me. And it's just as well I didn't know more, or I might have refused to do it for you!

Go Ape has two of Britain's longest zip wires, both over 400 metres long and 45 metres off the ground. And as if that isn't bad enough, they're over a rocky gorge, and all that's stopping you from falling is a safety harness.

Martin told me that my face, when we arrived, and I realised I was going to be flying through the air so high above the ground, was a picture – you know I have a terrible head for heights. He said I went sheet white!

You're a complete nutter, Nicole! Was there nothing that scared you?

Clearly life after a transplant was going to be all about thrill seeking and adventure in a way that life with cystic fibrosis never could be. Knowing that, there was no way I could back out, even though my knees had gone to jelly at the sight of the zip wires high in the sky.

First, we had to have a safety briefing, which didn't do much to quell my nerves – if it wasn't dangerous we wouldn't need this, I reckoned! I also got a bit distracted by a family that was there: a mum, a dad, two little girls aged around 10 and their younger brother. They reminded me of us, Nicole, and the family days we would have together, when we'd go bowling or to a local play park. We loved it when Dad was home from working away and we could all be together, the five of us. Watching them just reminded me that we'll never all be together again – something I still forget from time to time.

After we were kitted out with our safety harnesses, we climbed up to the platform where the zip wire started from. I made the mistake of looking down and immediately wished I hadn't: it was a *very* long way down.

Martin offered to go first to give me a bit more time to work up my courage. He took a short run along the platform then leapt into the air, shouting, 'Yahhoooooo!' as he flew down the wire to the platform opposite us. Show-off!

Then it was my turn.

'Why couldn't you have been less of a daredevil, Nicole?' I grumbled, as I took some deep breaths, my heart pounding so hard I thought it was going to jump out of my chest.

'Don't be nervous,' said the instructor, who was standing beside me. 'I promise you're going to love it. It's an incredible feeling.'

I wasn't convinced, but with other people waiting behind me it was now or never. 'This is for you, Nicole!' I said, blessing myself as I prepared to leap into the air.

Closing my eyes I jumped from the platform … and suddenly I was flying.

The sensation was amazing, like nothing I've ever experienced before. It must be how birds feel, completely free and weightless. You'd have *loved* it, sis.

It took me about 45 seconds to reach the other side, where Martin was waiting for me. 'That was amazing!' I exclaimed. 'I want to do it again!'

'You've changed your tune, haven't you?' he laughed, amused at my transformation from nervous wreck to daredevil.

From there we had to complete a gruelling course of ladders, bridges and swinging on ropes to get to the final zip wire, which would take us back to the start.

I went first this time. As I sailed back across the gorge I took in the incredible view of Loch Lomond spread out below me. From up so high, the world looks so peaceful and tranquil. If you're up above us somewhere, you definitely have the best seat in the house, Nicole.

Martin and I drove home, pumped full of adrenaline from our treetop adventure … but within minutes of sitting down on the sofa at home we were both fast asleep, exhausted from our energetic morning. And for the next three days we were both hobbling around like an old man and woman, because our muscles were so sore from all the exercise!

This wish definitely put me through my paces, Nicole, and has hopefully cured my fear of heights too!

'Learn To Swim'

There was one wish in particular that I couldn't do, which was learn to swim, because I already can.

I'd fretted over what to do about it for months then, late in 2013, I mentioned it to Gary and to my surprise he offered to take this one on for me.

'I've never been able to properly swim,' he admitted. 'I was always terrible at the lessons Mum sent us to when we were young and, being honest, I've always been a bit scared of the water, so I haven't got in a pool in years. But I'm going to Florida with Ayisha next year and I want to be able to swim for that. I'm 22 and it's something I should be able to do at my age!'

I was really taken aback by his honesty. You know Gary's not one to admit to weakness – he's a typical bloke in that respect. It must have taken a lot for him to tell me he couldn't swim.

While I was surprised by his confession, I'd always known you couldn't swim, Nicole. Even though Mum sent us for lessons at a local leisure centre when we were seven, and school took us swimming when we were 11, you just never got the hang of it. While I was one of the top swimmers in the class, you were the worst, and it used to really annoy you! It was nothing to do with cystic fibrosis – you just didn't seem to have the right co-ordination, while I was a real water baby.

Knowing how much Gary wanted to do this wish for you, I decided it wasn't cheating to let him take it on by himself. I offered to teach him and, six weeks ago, we went to a local pool together. But it was a disaster! He said I was bossy and had no patience, and ended up storming off to the changing rooms in a huff with me.

So, since then, he's been going with Ayisha. And last week he asked me to come and watch him swim.

I actually couldn't believe my eyes. From the man who could barely muster a doggy paddle and refused to get his face or head wet, now he's gliding through the water with a powerful stroke, looking like he's been swimming for years.

Standing in the warm water of the shallow end, watching him, I felt incredibly proud and I knew he had practised so hard so as not to let you down, Nicole.

You and he had such a typical big sister–little brother relationship. He would play pranks on you and wind you up, knowing just what buttons to press to get a reaction out of you. But you always made up quickly and you doted on him, spoiling him with presents and money if he was skint. And when I started working, and dating Martin, you and Gary became even closer because often it was just the two of you at home. Then, as you got sicker, your roles reversed and he was like your protector, taking you to the cinema or out for lunch, even carrying you to your bedroom if you were tired and not feeling well.

Although he doesn't share many of his feelings with us, I know how much he misses you. Throwing himself into learning to swim has been his way of paying tribute to you.

I was feeling quite emotional after watching him swim, but in typical Gary-the-joker fashion, he couldn't resist playing one of his pranks on me. He told me to go and stand in a certain part of the pool, but wouldn't tell me why. And, foolishly, I did. The next thing I knew, the wave machine had been turned on and I was swept off my feet! He let me flail about in the water for a moment or two, then swam up and grabbed me and we had a big hug in the middle of the pool, both of us laughing while I spat out mouthfuls of water!

When it comes to our baby bro, Nicole, some things never change!

Promise to write soon, 'Cole.

Love,

La La xxx

Letter Eleven
February 2015

Dear 'Cole,

I can hardly hold the pen to write this letter my hand is trembling so much with excitement. I'm crying, and my tears are dropping onto the paper, making the ink run. But for once these are happy tears.

Nicole, I'm getting married!!! Martin proposed this weekend and of course I said yes!

I can hardly believe it – I keep pinching myself, thinking it's all been a dream.

The final wish on your list was to get married, and when I read it, I thought it would be something I could do in the future. Since Martin and I met at a party in 2010 I've known I wanted to spend my future with him, but you know what boys are like – I thought he'd wait until we were older before he ever popped the question. Looks like I was wrong! I never imagined I'd be engaged so soon, but I'm so happy I am. And to be able to fulfil your last wish just makes it extra special.

'Get Married'

When Martin told me he was taking me away for a night to a mystery location, I was very excited and intrigued, but I actually thought he was trying to butter me up before he told me he'd booked a boys' holiday or something like that!

Patience has never been one of my strong points but luckily I've been so busy at work, the week flew by and before I knew it Friday had arrived, and it was time for our mystery mini-break.

Martin arrived at the house to pick me up. Before we left he asked Dad to come out and look at one of the tyres on his car, as he was worried it was a bit soft. Mum and I waited in the living room, my weekend bag at the door filled with a dressy outfit and heels for that evening, as Martin had told me we'd be going for a fancy meal.

'Where do you think he's taking me?' I asked Mum, while we waited.

'I've no idea, love, but I'm sure it'll be somewhere romantic. You deserve a lovely night away – you've been so busy working and getting through Nicole's list. Go and relax and enjoy yourself.'

Martin popped his head around the door. 'Ready to go?' he asked.

I jumped up from the sofa excitedly. ''Bye, Mum, 'bye, Dad,' I called, as we walked out of the house and got into the car.

'Have a great time!' Dad shouted. I noticed he had a very cheeky grin on his face but I was too excited as we hit the road to think much about it.

We drove out of Glasgow, towards Loch Lomond, and Martin put on a CD of all my favourite songs that he'd made for our road trip. As we sped down the motorway, music blasting, I felt some of the sadness that had overshadowed me begin to fade.

When I looked over at Martin, however, I noticed that he was pale and anxious looking. 'What's wrong? Are you OK?' I asked.

'Yeah, yeah, I'm fine. Just got some work stuff on my mind,' he replied distractedly.

Soon we pulled into the car park of a luxury hotel called The Lodge On The Loch, right on the shores of Loch Lomond.

'Oh, my God,' I squealed, 'I've wanted to stay here for years!'

'I know – you've dropped enough hints to me! Why do you think I picked it?' Martin laughed, lifting our bags out of the boot.

Nicole, you would have *loved* the room we checked into: crisp white bed linen, fancy toiletries in the bathroom and the most stunning view over the water. It was so luxurious.

'I've got a present here for you,' Martin said, clearing his throat nervously.

'A present?' I replied, totally confused.

'Well, I only got you some perfume for your Valentine's present this year, so this is to make up for that.'

He handed me a bundle of envelopes with a note on top which read: 'Here are 12 tokens of Martin's love for you, one for every month of the year. Use them wisely or you'll be punished in the form of tickling!'

One by one I opened the envelopes. Inside each one was a message typed on a piece of paper, promising a different date: 'A safari date … a shoe shopping date … a dinner date …' I burst into tears as I read them, so overwhelmed at how sweet and thoughtful he'd been.

'And there's one more type of date I'd like us to have, Melissa,' he said, getting down on one knee and producing a small, velvet-covered box from his pocket. 'I love you and I want us to have a wedding date. Will you marry me, Melissa Tennant?'

I swear I couldn't speak a word, Nicole! I was frozen to the spot in shock. Eventually I managed to stutter out, 'Yes … yes!' and I threw my arms around him, crying my eyes out but laughing with happiness at the same time.

It's been so long since I've felt this happy, Nicole. For so long, worry about your health, and then grief at your death, has ruled my emotions. But in that moment, held tightly in Martin's arms, with a beautiful diamond and tanzanite ring on my left hand, I felt completely carefree.

Martin explained he'd bought the ring a few days before, with some help from his sister, and had asked Dad's permission earlier that day when they'd been looking at the tyre on his car.

'I just can't believe it …' I kept saying over and over, unable to take my eyes off my ring.

Once I'd calmed down a bit, I immediately phoned home.

Dad had told Mum the second we'd driven off, so they were expecting the call, and hearing how happy they were was amazing. 'You deserve your happiness, Melissa,' Mum said tearfully – I knew they were happy tears. 'Grab hold of it and never let it go. We are so thrilled for you. I can't believe my baby girl is going to be a bride!'

That evening we went for a romantic meal in the hotel's restaurant but we were both too excited to eat a bite. Our steaks sat untouched on the plates as we talked nonstop about wedding plans and our honeymoon, and looking for our first home together.

And it was then, Nicole, that I realised, with all my excitement and happiness at getting engaged, that you wouldn't be a part of any of these plans. I felt a stab of guilt that I hadn't thought about that sooner, and I know you'll understand that I just got caught up in the moment. But once I'd started thinking about you, I couldn't stop. I should have been able to call you to ask if you'd be my maid of honour, and knowing you, you would probably have come straight to the hotel to celebrate with us! You'd have appointed yourself my wedding planner, making mood boards of fabric samples, filing away images ripped from bridal magazines and ensuring the colour scheme for the bridesmaids suited your colouring. We could have gone shopping for my dress together, with Mum, spending a happy Saturday in posh bridal shops as I tried on beautiful gowns. And I'd have happily let you take charge of it all, knowing how creative you were and how happy it would have made you. I realised too that you won't be there on my wedding morning to calm my nerves before Dad walks me down the aisle, and someone else will have to be my witness and sign the wedding register after the ceremony.

I knew Martin would understand completely but I kept all these thoughts private from him that night. I didn't want this gentle sadness to cast any shadow over his happiness when he'd worked so hard to make everything perfect for me.

I've no doubt in my mind you'd approve of having Martin as a brother-in-law. From the first day I brought him home, you told me he was a keeper. And that was so important to me – I could never have been with someone you didn't like. And he's more than proven himself in these last few years. I honestly don't know what I'd have done without him supporting me through losing you; he's been my rock, and while other guys might have run a mile when faced with so much pain and sadness, he's never let me down.

You and him got on like a house on fire, you were like brother and sister, and I know he misses you terribly as well.

When we started talking about who we'd have in the bridal party, at first I thought I wouldn't have any bridesmaids. If I couldn't have you, I didn't want anyone. But then I thought about the girls who've helped me since we lost you, and who loved you so much. And I realised having them there with me would help me feel closer to you. So I've chosen Katrina, Alice, Rhiannon, Alana and Martin's sister, Laura. Of course, none of them will be as good a bridesmaid as you would have been, but I hope you approve!

We've set the date as 14 August 2016, and chosen Dalmeny Park Country House Hotel as the venue. Dad is ridiculously excited at the thought of giving me away and puffs his chest out with pride every time anyone asks about the wedding. Mum's already on the hunt for her hat, would you believe!

We haven't made any other plans but one thing I know for sure is that on the day, I'll insist on being driven to your grave for a few moments to lay my bouquet on it. If you can't be there and have your own, then you can have mine, Nicole.

And it's strange thinking my wedding will be in the same month as the anniversary of your death. It wasn't a deliberate decision, but the more I think about it, the more I believe it's a good one. You would have been the first to say life has to go on, and while July will always be hard for everyone, I hope my wedding and its anniversary in the years ahead will give some balance to the pain that month will always hold for us.

I was looking at photos of us from our First Communion Day today, Nicole – when we walked proudly up the aisle of the church together, hand in hand, in our beautiful white dresses. Remember how excited we were and how beautiful we felt? We were so innocent then, with no idea about what lay ahead of us. I'm going to tuck a photo of us both into my dress on the day, so a part of you will once again make that journey up the aisle with me.

You were beside me then. Please be at my side on my wedding day. I know you can't be there in body, Nicole, but you're my maid of honour in spirit, and I only hope I can plan this wedding as beautifully as you would have done for me.

Miss you so much today, twinny,

La La xxx

Epilogue
March 2015

Dear 'Cole,

It's finished. I can hardly believe it.

Your list of wishes that I found 18 months ago, the night before your funeral, is now complete.

There are so many emotions surging through me right now. Relief that I've done it – it hasn't been easy at times, and I've put myself under so much pressure to tick off every wish, doing each one just the way you would have wanted. And then there's happiness – I've made your dreams come true, Nicole, every one of them. It was the very last thing I could do for you as your twin, and I'm so happy I've been able to. Your wishes have seen me grow in confidence, travel to countries I might never have visited and overcome my own fears and anxieties. I'm a different person now, so much braver and able to seize the moment. That's been your final gift to me, Nicole. But, mixed up with my relief and happiness, there's fear and sadness.

Your wishes have kept you close to me, and held at bay the awful reality that you've gone and you're never coming back.

They've been my link with you all these months since you died. Now they're all complete, I know that I have to let you go and that is so hard to contemplate. Without your list, what will keep my mind busy, and stop me falling back into my grief?

I'm scared, Nicole.

So, inspired by you, sis, I've drawn up my own bucket list, to keep me busy in the years ahead without you.

1. Raise £10,000 for The Butterfly Trust, which I have set up in your memory to offer respite care to young people with cystic fibrosis, and their families.
2. If Martin and I have a daughter one day, name her Nicole after you and tell her how amazing her aunt was.
3. See a cure for cystic fibrosis discovered in my lifetime.

Those are my wishes, each one a connection with you, and I'm as determined to make them come true as I have been to fulfil yours.

I know, though, that I have to let you go now.

I hope that knowing all your dreams have come true gives you peace, Nicole, and that wherever you are, there's no more pain or illness for you now.

Whenever the pain of missing you becomes too much to bear, I'm going to remember the words I have tattooed on my back in your memory.

'*You are my sun, my moon and all my stars.*'

You were, and still are, my everything, Nicole. My sister, my partner in crime, my bestest friend.

I will love you for ever, 'Cole.

Goodbye.

La La xxx

Acknowledgements

I'd like to thank everyone at Ebury, particularly my editors Kelly Ellis and Anna Mrowiec, for giving me this fantastic opportunity. Thanks also to Eimear O'Hagan, for piecing together my story and helping me create a lasting legacy for Nicole.

I couldn't have done this without my parents, who are two of my best friends and greatest supporters, and the help of the rest of my friends and family. They picked me up when I thought I couldn't complete the list. Special thanks to Laura, Kelly, Gary, Paul, Kat and Alana.

And lastly Martin, who has been my strength. I can't really put into words how much you mean to me; all I can say is that I can't wait to get married and spend the rest of my life with you.

A note from Melissa ...

If you have been moved by Nicole's story, please register for organ donation in her memory, and one day you may be able to save a life like hers. You can sign up in a number of ways:

- You could fill out a form on the NHS website: www. organdonation.nhs.uk
- You can call the NHS donor line on 0300 123 23 23
- Or you can also join when you register at your GP surgery, or for a driving licence, for a European Health Insurance card, or even when you apply for a Boots Advantage card.

I'd also like to urge you to support the fantastic work that The Butterfly Trust does, providing face-to-face practical support to people living with cystic fibrosis and their families. I don't know where we'd have been without them.

You can visit their website, www.butterflytrust.org.uk, to find out more.

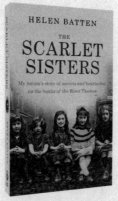